organic

BABY AND TODDLER COOKBOOK

organic

BABY AND TODDLER COOKBOOK

Lizzie Vann of *Organix*

Photography by
Simon Brown

DK

LONDON, NEW YORK, MUNICH
MELBOURNE, DELHI

Project Editors: Nasim Mawji, Sue Cooper

Art Editors: Toni Kay, Vicki Groombridge

Designer: Poppy Jenkins

DTP Designer: Conrad van Dyke

Deputy Art Director: Carole Ash

Production Manager: Maryann Webster

Food Stylist: Susie Theodorou
assisted by Jaqueline Malouf

Jacket Designer: Neal Cobourne

First published in Great Britain in 2000
by Dorling Kindersley Limited
80 Strand, London WC2 ORL

A Penguin Company

A CIP catalogue record for this book is
available from the British Library

ISBN-13: 978-1-4053-1964-5
ISBN-10: 1-4053-1964-X

*Although there is usually no need to peel organic fruit and
vegetables, they should be peeled for children under ten months of
age as their fibrous skins can be difficult to digest.*

Reproduced by Colourscan (Singapore)
Printed and bound in Singapore by Tien Wah Press

Printed on acid-free, chlorine-free, recyclable
and biodegradable paper from a sustainable
forestry source

Discover more at
www.dk.com

Why organic?

A child's delicate physiology
makes him especially vulnerable
to the toxic elements in food; this
chapter explains how an organic
diet can give your child a better
start in life.

What is organic?

A look at the ever-expanding
array of organic ingredients
available locally and from around
the world; the benefits of organic
farming for farmers, animals and
the environment.

Recipes

Health issues and nutrition

Introduction

I believe that there is nothing more important than the quality of the food that we feed our children – their development, health and happiness depend on it. This book has been created to give you lots of ideas for making meal-times a success. It features simple, classic recipes, tried and tested on hundreds of children.

Children like to have fun. They like new ideas, new colours and new flavours. Many food manufacturers and cookery writers have responded to this by disguising food with lots of bright colours and masking its real flavour with excessive sugar or salt, even arranging it into shapes such as boats or teddy bears.

Since setting up Organix in 1992, my approach has been first and foremost to make sure that we have the fundamentals of good food right and that we focus on these above all else. These fundamentals are explained in more detail in the first chapters of this book, but in essence they are:

• Always use organic ingredients because they are better for your child in many ways.
• Always use natural ingredients in simple combinations – these offer the best nutrition and the best flavour.

Good food is important to children. They

• Keep sugar and processed ingredients out of your child's diet for as long as possible. The early years are critical in building a library of flavours that your child will draw upon later in life, and natural, unprocessed foods will teach children to appreciate the real taste of food. Good-quality ingredients do not need added sugar, salt or stock cubes.

• Do not add artificial colourings to food – you don't need to when you can use the wonderful vivid colours of strawberries, citrus fruits or peppers, for example. Most children love eating – the food is entertainment itself and even the faddy ones will enjoy some foods.

• Make meal-times more fun by talking about food and sharing your time and your childrens' enjoyment. They will not need funny shapes to entertain them if they have your attention.

• Encourage an interest in where food comes from and how it is grown, as this will help children to appreciate it. Older children will enjoy getting involved in preparing food and even visiting farms and gardens.

Organix receives calls from over 20,000 parents each year. Their passion for ensuring that their children eat good food comes across in the recipes they share with us, but also in their stories about visits to farms and local gardens and cookery classes that have been set up in local nursery schools.

Good food is important to children. They take pleasure in it; they need it. I hope that this book will help both you and your children to enjoy meal-times even more.

Lizzie Vann

take *pleasure* in it; they *need* it.

why ORGANIC?

Organic food not only offers your child

the very best start in life – it also offers

a better future for the world in which

your child will grow.

The best *for* your baby

Nothing is more important for your baby than safe, healthy food. All children deserve the best possible nourishment, and to be protected from harmful elements that may damage them.

HOW A CHILD'S BODY DEVELOPS

The most rapid growth periods are in the uterus, during infancy and at puberty:

• A baby grows about 50cm (20in) in his first year and by 2 years old has reached half of his adult height; at puberty he has a growth spurt of 12cm (5in) per year

• At birth, 14% of a baby's body weight is fat; by 6 months this rises to 25%; a 2-year-old weighs 20% of his adult weight; an 11-year-old is half of his adult weight.

Hardly a week passes without another food scare hitting the headlines. Concerns about genetically modified (GM) foods, bovine spongiform encephalopathy (BSE) and pesticides are just some of the major issues that have caused anxious parents to search for safer, more wholesome food for their children.

Existing regulations are based on 'acceptable' levels for adult consumption and may not protect children from toxins. Babies and young children are at greater risk because the immaturity of their organs and body systems makes them more vulnerable to toxins. Children also receive higher exposure to pesticides from the limited types of foods they eat.

The only way to avoid these threats to your child's health is to ensure that everything he eats and drinks is organic, pesticide- and additive-free and grown in conditions that are regulated and monitored. More and more parents are deciding that there should be no compromise on what they feed their babies.

Why children are vulnerable

From conception until one year of age children are at their most vulnerable. During this critical stage of development cells are multiplying at their peak, yet the body has a limited diet to draw upon. In addition, immature organs and body systems respond differently to food – a baby's digestive system is more efficient than that of an adult at absorbing foods, enabling nutrients to be used more quickly but making the baby more vulnerable to toxins. Also, immature kidneys are not as proficient at excreting harmful substances, so they may circulate in the body for longer. Research cannot be relied upon as processed foods and chemicals are tested on adults, and scaling down the results for infants won't necessarily give an accurate answer. Also, babies eat far more per kilogram of body weight than adults and their fluid intake is far higher.

Pesticides are a cause for concern, particularly since research has revealed their presence in breast milk, a baby's first food. They have been found to bind to fat and once absorbed may stay in the body for a lifetime, some emerging in milk during breast-feeding. Despite this, all experts still recommend breast-feeding as best. Breast milk is the ultimate superfood, produced to satisfy your baby's specific needs.

THE RISK TO CHILDREN

A child's body composition makes him vulnerable because:

• Vital organs develop throughout childhood; a child's immature kidneys are less able to filter out harmful substances and cannot break down some toxins

• The nervous system grows rapidly in the first year and continues until the age of 18; its development can be disrupted by exposure to toxins

• Until the age of 6, a child's body is made up of more water and less fat than that of an adult; fats, which in an adult 'trap' and store pesticide residues, are less able to do this job, leaving them to circulate in the body; water-soluble pesticides are also more able to circulate in a child's body.

Protect your children's health by ensuring that everything they eat and drink is organic and free from artificial additives.

READING FOOD LABELS

Food can only be labelled 'organic' if at least 95% of its ingredients are organic. Rules applying to organic food are legally defined and recognized by European Union (EU) standards. Read labels carefully, and know what to look out for:

• A valid organic certification symbol, such as that of the Soil Association in the UK

• The list of the food's constituents: the first ingredient listed is the product's largest constituent; the amount of other ingredients reduces as you read on

• The percentage of each ingredient in processed foods; EU regulations on the need to declare these came into force in early 2000; some companies just show the percentage of the ingredients shown in the food title, however many organic food companies show the percentage of all ingredients.

Pesticide residues

For the first four to six months, babies are dependent upon breast or formula milk for their nourishment. Recent research, carried out by a team from Leeds University in the UK, revealed that over 350 chemicals accumulate in women's body fat and can be passed on to breast-fed babies. Despite this, breast milk is still recognized as the ideal babyfood, superior to infant formula, which is cow's milk modified to approximate the nutritional profile of breast milk.

Babies' first foods are usually starchy and easy to purée as they are intended to smooth the transition between fluids and solids. Fruit and vegetables figure highly in the diet and research has shown that unless these come from certified organic sources, they often harbour traces of pesticide residues. A 1998 survey by the Ministry of Agriculture, Fisheries and Foods (MAFF) found small levels of residues in 10 per cent of a sample of babyfoods on sale in the UK and higher levels of residues in many of the common fruit and vegetables used to make babyfood at home.

American studies into pesticide residues in the diets of infants and children were carried out by the National Research Council in 1993. They concluded that because these groups ate far more of a smaller variety of certain foods, especially fruit juices and puréed fresh fruit and vegetables, they were at greater risk than adults from the effects of pesticides.

Growing awareness of food quality is already changing eating habits. In 1999, over 30 per cent of the population regularly bought some organic fruits or vegetables, and more than 1 in 3 parents reported giving their baby some organic babyfood.

Additives

Many processed foods – sausages, burgers, confectionery and drinks such as squash, for example – contain an alarming number of additives in the form of chemical preservatives, antioxidants, stabilizers, thickeners, flavour enhancers and colourings. The UK Food Commission estimates that consumers may ingest up to 60 additives from just one convenience

Many *additives* have been found to cause or

meal. Over 50 of the additives looked at had to some degree been linked to health problems in some people, including allergic asthma, eczema, birth deformities and cancer. Such additives can be approved for use in the UK because the research has not been proven in each member state of the European Community.

There is evidence that certain additives are unsuitable for some sensitive people, and many additives have been found to cause or aggravate allergic reactions and contribute to hyperactivity in children. The biggest culprits are the 'E numbers'. Many of them are banned in baby and toddler foods, but they may be present in 'family foods' that you might feed to your child.

Genetic Modification

Genetically modified (GM) organisms are another major concern for parents wishing to protect their children. Scientists are now able to transfer genes between organisms, thus changing the characteristics of the host organism. Genes from soil bacteria have been inserted into soya beans to make them resistant to herbicides, genes from fish have been inserted into tomatoes to prolong their shelf-life and genes from bacteria have been inserted into maize to kill pests, which may damage the butterfly population. Many people feel that there has been insufficient research into the long-term effects of genetic modification – on wildlife and on humans. Because the technology requires the use of antibiotic-resistant genes, there is concern that their ingestion will increase antibiotic resistance in people.

In the same way that the special physiology of babies makes them more vulnerable to pesticide residues, we suspect that GM foods may have a greater impact on children compared to adults. The only way to protect yourself and your baby is to eat organic.

ADDITIVES TO AVOID

Babyfoods are covered by special legislation. Preservatives, colourings and added salt are forbidden because babies cannot process them. However babyfood may contain other ingredients that can be a cause for concern. Check the label for the following:

• Sugars, including sucrose, dextrose, glucose, fructose, lactose, maltose and honey or fruit syrups; use of these sweeteners can indicate that not enough higher-quality ingredients such as fruit are present

• Meat or vegetable extracts, hydrolysed vegetable protein or yeast in savoury foods, which could indicate overprocessing

• Flavourings; these are unnecessary in babyfoods and introduce your child to artificial tastes

• Processing aids such as emulsifiers and demineralized whey; all organic baby foods are produced without these ingredients

• Processed starches, including modified corn flour, maltodextrin, rice starch and wheat starch; these often accompany the over-use of water; they are low-nutrient fillers that dull the flavour of food and take up the space of more nutritious ingredients.

aggravate *allergic reactions* in children

**ENCOURAGING AN
INTEREST IN FOOD**

Teach your child to enjoy good
food made with fresh, organic
ingredients. The following tips
can help to encourage healthy
eating habits for life:

• Involve your child in the
preparation and cooking of
meals – cooking builds a sense
of pride in achievement and
even young children can stir
currants into a fruit cake; the
kitchen and your child will
probably get messy, but both
can be scrubbed down

• Encourage your child to
experiment with recipes and
different ingredients as he gets
older and grows in confidence;
the results will help him to
learn more about nutrition,
taste, smell and texture

• Buy a juicer and experiment
with different fruit and vegetable
combinations; encourage your
child to invent his own favourite
juice recipes.

The benefits of organic for your child

Every parent wants his or her child to have the best possible start in life.
Parents instinctively know that an infant is vulnerable in ways that older
children and adults are not. Surveys have shown that young children eat
a lot more unrefined food, weight for weight, than adults. The types and
purity of the food they eat can have a bigger impact upon them than on
adults. As children's bodies grow and develop – the reproductive system,
for example, develops until the age of 20 – they are more susceptible to
the quality of their environment, including their food.

Organic food is grown without artificial pesticides. Unnecessary
farming and processing chemicals are not used. There are careful rules
about the way ingredients can be processed and additives such as
flavourings and colourings are not allowed. In organic food production,
strict standards will have been followed and monitored. Animals will not
have been given hormones or antibiotics, which means that you will
never find residues of these in the meat, a concern for some as there
have been fears that years of consumption of low levels of antibiotics
can have a detrimental effect on the immune system.

Many health problems in young children have been linked to a poorly
functioning immune system. Although the causes of this are not clear,
feeding babies organic food will not contribute to this problem, but will
help to build a strong immune system and make children more resistant
to disease. An organic diet sows the seeds of good health, which can be
nurtured throughout your child's life, influencing his or her food choices
and preferences. Eating organic food also safeguards your child's fertility,
enabling him or her to pass on good health to the next generation.

The benefits of organic for all the family

Although reasons for buying organic vary, health is probably top of
the list. There is now substantial evidence that residues left in food by
artificial pesticides and other chemicals can be harmful. Although the
reasons why are unclear, a Danish study showed that sperm counts in

Unnecessary farming and processing *chemicals*

Western men have dropped dramatically over the past 50 years. In contrast, a 1994 article in *The Lancet* reported that organic farmers and growers who ate organic produce had sperm counts that were nearly 50 per cent higher than men working in other professions who did not.

It is difficult to prove that organic food has higher nutritional values than conventional food, but produce does contain fewer nitrates and pesticides, less water and can have higher vitamin C and mineral levels. Many people believe that organic food tastes better. So many processed foods contain artificial flavourings or processing aids to make them 'smoother' or 'spreadable' that it is becoming difficult to define the real taste of food. Eating organically is also healthier on the basis that you are avoiding hydrogenated fat, artificial additives and artificial preservatives. I am convinced that since we began to eat organic a few years ago, my family and I have enjoyed better health and a greater zest for life.

are not used in organic food

GROW YOUR OWN

You can grow your own fruit and vegetables in anything from a plant pot to a fully fledged organic vegetable garden. Even the smallest members of the family will enjoy planting seeds and watching them grow. Try the following:

• Sprout beans, seeds and peas indoors on windowsills; they are highly nutritious and add a wonderful crunch to lunch box sandwiches and salads

• Grow herbs at home (see page 64); children are fascinated by the smell released when they rub the leaves of fragrant herbs such as basil or sage.

**WHERE TO BUY
ORGANIC PRODUCTS**

The more you request and buy organic fruit and vegetables and other products, the more easily available they will become. Currently:

• Most large supermarkets stock some organic products

• Some organic supermarkets sell organic cosmetics, pet food, environmentally-friendly household cleaners, clothes and books promoting an organic lifestyle, as well as the widest range of organic foods

• Farm shops and farmer's markets are a good source of fresh fruit and vegetables if you live nearby

• Organic box schemes and mail order companies can deliver the best produce to your door; box schemes are usually operated by the grower, or a group of farmers who pool their crops and send out boxes of freshly harvested seasonal fruit and vegetables (see pages 140–41)

• Many companies now market their produce on the internet (see pages 140–41).

It's a family affair

Making sweeping changes can be unpopular and might harden cynical attitudes held by other members of the family. Start introducing organic foods gradually so that the family has time to accept and appreciate the differences. Discuss the benefits of organic food at meal-times and listen to what is important to other members of your family when they talk about the foods they like to eat. You might need to be patient where their favourite convenience foods are concerned or clever in finding acceptable alternatives. But there are an increasing number of organic foods that can give you both peace of mind and peace at the dinner table. Organic pizza, for instance, is now available both in the shops and in some restaurant chains. And there is a growing range of tinned organic foods such as tomatoes and baked beans, which are hugely popular in the UK and US.

A good place to begin your conversion programme is with foods you eat often or have particular concerns about (see pages 18–19). Organic bread, milk, cheese, carrots and potatoes can be found in most large supermarkets. Look at what is available when you go shopping. You might need to seek out the 'organic aisle' as supermarkets often put all their organic produce together rather than with food of the same type. Over the next few years we should begin to see many more organic foods taking their place in the 'normal' shelves alongside conventional foods.

Try to bring home something new every week, perhaps something for the storecupboard such as baking products, dried fruit, nuts, herbs, spices, pasta or rice. Organic treats such as chocolate, cakes, biscuits and ice cream might help to soften the sceptics, but you could try to use the change in your family's diet to enforce the principles of healthy eating as well as substituting organic for conventional foods.

Why not make sure that there are plenty of organic yoghurts in the refrigerator and a fruit bowl brimming over with luscious organic fruits? You could also use this opportunity to start introducing some more unusual fruits and vegetables.

With *organic* ingredients you know that what

Organics on a budget

When we do have to pay more for organic food, it is for the simple reason that it has cost more to produce (see page 24). Many would argue that that little extra is a small price to pay for quality and peace of mind, and in fact, prices are dropping all the time as more consumers demand organic products. Try some of the following money-saving tips for reducing any expense involved in going organic:

• Identify five foods that make regular appearances on your shopping list and try to find affordable organic alternatives

• Look out for organic supermarket own-brand items which are often cheaper than branded non-organic products

• Replace conventional lettuce (notorious for high pesticide residues) with organic white and red cabbage in salads; children often prefer its crunchier texture

• Buy organic fruit and vegetables when in season (see pages 138–39); make the most of summer fruits and winter root crops

• Take advantage of special offers; buy in bulk and freeze what you cannot use

• Check out the freezer cabinet in your supermarket; frozen vegetables are often more nutritious and frozen organic vegetables are cheaper than their fresh counterparts

• Grow your own organic herbs (see pages 140–41)

• Use your organic fruit and vegetable waste on your organic compost heap.

you get is a *real taste*

ORGANIC CERTIFICATION IN THE UK

Several inspection bodies have been approved by the UK Register of Organic Food Standards to ensure that farms wishing to market organic products are thoroughly inspected and maintain the high standards required.

Certification enables farms to label produce with a symbol of certification. This guarantees that a farmer has followed an approved organic production and processing system that has been verified by a team of independent inspectors.

In the UK, over 80% of organic foods are certified by the Soil Association.

CHOOSE ORGANIC

The UK Ministry of Agriculture, Farming and Fisheries (MAFF) tests UK and imported non-organic fruit and vegetables for residues of toxic pesticides. Excluding these fruit and vegetables from your baby or child's diet is one way to reduce his exposure to pesticides, but a far better approach is to choose organic fruit and vegetables wherever possible. The following list shows the percentage of samples tested where pesticide residues were detected in 2002 and 2003:

- Oranges 97%
- Apples 80%
- Pears 79%
- Celery 72%
- Strawberries 71%
- Grapes 62%
- Peaches 61%
- Raspberries 57%
- Lettuce 32%
- Carrots 2%

A guide to organic ingredients

Uniformity of size and shape is not the best way to judge any food. Rely more on smell, flavour and freshness. Even the best organic produce may not be blemish-free and the odd insect may be found between the leaves. These imperfections should be celebrated because they indicate a lack of artificial fertilizers, pesticides and other chemical intervention in your food. Here are some of the most important organic products to buy:

Fruit and vegetables

Of all the food groups, fruit and vegetables have the highest pesticide residues, and buying organic is the best way to avoid them. Seasonal, naturally grown and harvested produce is more flavoursome. Look into organic box schemes (see pages 140–41): they deliver seasonal fresh fruit and vegetables to your door.

Milk and dairy products

These are some of the biggest organic sellers in supermarkets. Organic milk differs from the conventional pint because the cows feed on organic pastures, hay and silage, have freedom to roam and do not suffer the indignities of prophylactic drugs and other treatments designed to maximize their yields to unacceptable levels. Organic dairies tend to be smaller concerns; the milk and other dairy products they produce have a purity that can be relied upon, and a noticeably sweeter, cleaner flavour.

Meat and poultry

Organically farmed varieties are now widely available, offering more humanely produced alternatives to conventionally force-fed creatures that are routinely injected with growth hormones and antibiotics. Scares such as BSE have prompted public questioning and a wave of abhorrence against farming methods that include unnatural foodstuffs for animals. Organic farms operate strict regulations and consider the welfare of their stock as well as production. A better life for stock, humane slaughtering and good butchery techniques give an organic end product better flavour. Often with lower water contents, organic meats also shrink less during cooking so they go further and have a better texture. Both chickens reared for meat and for egg production live a more natural life, unlike their caged cousins.

Fish Much of the fish available today has been reared in fish farms. This means that they will have been caged underwater, fed an unnatural diet and treated with pesticides to prevent the spread of disease. Organic fish – especially salmon and trout – is increasingly available. The fish are reared in high-quality water, fed the same diet that they would eat in the wild and are not subjected to pesticides or artificial treatments.

Bread and flour Cereal crops are regularly sprayed with pesticides that collect in the grain's outer layers, raising concerns about residues in bread, cakes and biscuits. The lack of artificial additives in an organic loaf, from dough conditioners to chemical improvers, gives the bread a more wholesome flavour and texture. There is also a wide range of organic pasta available.

Oils and butter Organic vegetable oils are produced from organic crops and are pressed, not solvent-extracted, a process that can introduce toxic molecules. The increasing risk of genetically modified (GM) products being used in oils is one very good reason to seek out organic labels, all of which exclude GM ingredients. In 1996, over half the UK butter samples tested contained traces of lindane, a proven carcinogen.

COOKING ORGANIC FRUIT AND VEGETABLES

There is no better way to enjoy the full nutritional value of organic fruit and vegetables than to eat them raw. Where cooking is preferred, you may even find that your favourite recipes taste better. Try the following tips:

• Reduce the cooking time; food loses its nutrients from the time it is harvested, but this loss speeds up during cooking, and high temperatures accelerate the process

• Lightly steam or stir-fry vegetables – they will taste and look better than boiled ones

• Use a blender to make healthy purées, soups and sauces

• Find out about organic cookery courses.

There is no better way to enjoy the full nutritional value of organic fruit and vegetables than to eat them raw

As nature
intended

ORGANIC FARM VISITS

A visit to an organic farm provides a good opportunity to learn about where food comes from and how it is produced. It can also be an enjoyable day out. There are organizations that can put you in touch with organic farms that are open to the public (see pages 140–41). Children might like to do some of the following on a farm visit:

• Watch how cows are milked and feel the suction of a milking machine on their fingers

• Learn about what the different animals eat and help feed them

• See how various crops grow and help to pick or harvest them

• Enjoy a picnic in the countryside – you may be able to buy some of your food from the farm shop.

N.B. Farms that are open to the public should have hand-washing facilities; always make sure that children wash their hands before leaving the farm.

Organic farming relies on the principle of sustainability. To ensure that our resources are there for the next generation, whatever is taken from the soil must be returned and its health must be looked after.

Farmers build fertility into the soil using animal manures, remains of spent crops and natural rock and vegetable extracts. They rotate crops to avoid exhausting the soil and outwit weeds using mechanical means rather than sprays. The use of artificial fertilizers and pesticides is forbidden, and natural predators are encouraged as a means of controlling disease. It takes at least two years for a conventional farm to build natural fertility, allow pesticide residues to diminish and become recognized as organic.

The benefits of organic for farmers

More farm workers are needed on organic farms than on conventional farms as more tasks are carried out manually than by machine, and animals are cared for by stockmen and women who have regular contact with them. This human link helps to retain jobs in the countryside, keeping together village communities, and it also helps us to stay in touch with a fundamental part of our lives – that of food production.

Farmers who farm conventionally using artificial chemicals (many of which were developed from chemical warfare in the Second World

Animals on organic farms are fed with a varied, often organic diet – they are not fed animal products, drugs or antibiotics.

War), may be putting themselves at risk simply because so little is known about the long-term effects they can have on the environment, people and animals. Despite protestations from chemical companies about the safety of their products if used correctly, the instructions are often hard or impossible to follow in the field.

Caring for animals

In conventional agriculture animals are too often treated as components in the food chain. They may be reared in cramped conditions that are

not compatible with their physiology and instinctive behaviour, and as a result are more prone to disease. To combat this, they may be routinely given antibiotics – a practice causing concern amongst doctors who fear this may contribute to the growth in antibiotic resistance amongst humans. On organic farms, herbal and homeopathic treatments are used and it is only if the animal fails to respond to these that it is withdrawn from the organic system and treated conventionally. Livestock is kept in far kinder conditions on organic farms, where freedom to roam is a high priority. Free range access to pasture and good housing reduces stress levels, thereby strengthening an animal's natural immunity and reducing susceptibility to disease. Animals are well looked after and fed with a varied, often organic diet, not fed animal products, drugs or antibiotics.

A food system that destroys wildlife ignores the ecosystem and the way that life works.

ORGANIC CERTIFICATION AROUND THE WORLD

If a food has been produced outside the UK, in order to be certified organic in the UK the standards used have to be inspected and approved by one of the UK certifiers such as the Soil Association.

Worldwide bodies such as the International Federation of Organic Agricultural Movements (IFOAM) exist to:

• Promote and improve organic food and farming standards

• Make sure that what is organic in one country meets the standards of organic inspection in another.

Where our food comes from

More than 80 per cent of fruit and vegetables and over 70 per cent of organic foods overall are imported into the UK. When you choose organic food you are supporting small farmers all over the world. The five ingredients that feature most prominently in a baby's diet are all produced organically and readily available:

Milk You should choose your milk carefully, for your own sake and for that of your child. The purity (or impurity) of the milk that you drink can be transferred to your child in your breast milk, so to protect your child it is important to drink organic milk yourself. Traces of lindane, a pesticide that has been linked with cancer if consumed over a long period of time, have been found in conventional milk. Organic milk is now available in most supermarkets. Nearly two-thirds of organic dairy products on sale in the UK are produced here and include a wide range of yoghurts, cheeses, cream and ice cream.

Apples One of the most difficult fruits to grow organically because of the range of pests and diseases that can affect them, apples are grown successfully in the UK, Italy, Australia and the US. Organic farmers grow disease-resistant varieties and introduce natural predators such as ladybirds to deal with pests. They do not wax the fruit in the way that conventional producers do; the shiny, blemish-free apple may look the

best, but it could have harmful insecticide, fungicide or herbicide residues sealed into it. Some of these pesticides wash off in the rain, but others are sealed in with wax and can only be removed by peeling.

Oranges Pesticide residues were found in every supermarket- and shop-bought orange during government tests in the UK in 1999 – 68 per cent contained three or more chemicals, 40 per cent four or more, and many had five or six. Search out organic oranges and juice from Spain, Portugal, Italy, Israel, Australia and the US. You can also find organic orange juice made from organic orange juice concentrate.

Bananas The most popular fruit in the UK and a common weaning food, bananas are the fifth most important food commodity worldwide. Look for organic bananas from Brazil and the Windward Islands. They are planted far enough apart to prevent the spread of disease and grown with plants such as acacia trees, which fix nitrogen and naturally fertilize the soil. In contrast, Costa Rica, a leading banana producer and exporter, is the world's largest user of agrochemicals per head of population.

Rice In China, rice changed from being extensively farmed to intensively farmed in the 1960s with the introduction of synthetic fertilizers. Years later, farmers are concerned that the land is getting more compacted and more difficult to work and blame it on the use of artificial chemicals. They say that the rice is harder and does not taste as good. Rice, along with wheat, is one of the most heavily sprayed crops so it is worth looking for organic brands in order to safeguard your child from the residues that may be present in non-organic varieties.

FAIR TRADE

Fair-trade goods are not necessarily organic, but there is often overlap. Organic standards bodies are considering adopting fair-trade principles which ensure that food is produced under conditions that are most beneficial to workers. They aim to:

• Protect workers from exposure to high levels of pesticides and chemicals

• Provide clean water

• Provide good living conditions

• Pay above-average wages

• Provide welfare, education and medical aid.

**JUSTIFYING
THE EXPENSE**

When organic food costs more (and this is not always the case), higher prices reflect the care taken in its production:

• Yields are lower because they are not artificially enhanced using growth hormones and synthetic fertilizers

• Animals are reared in humane conditions with care taken to respect their welfare; this means that both land and labour costs are higher than in conventional farming

• Organic farmers and food companies are usually smaller than their conventional counterparts; they produce in smaller quantities and as a result have none of the financial advantages of bulk buying or economies of scale

• The testing regimes to ensure that foods are pesticide- and GM-free can be a financial burden for organic food companies.

Organics around the world

Sustainable and organic foods are grown for two reasons – either because they are part of a natural farming system that has been in use for centuries; or because public concern has pressurized farmers into adopting a more natural system of farming where they had previously practised an industrial style of agriculture. Generally the food is produced by reassuringly small concerns where attention to detail is a way of life. Sustainable, organic farming is practised all over the world and is well established in many countries.

The US is the largest producer of organic food with sales worth over US$7 billion a year, driven by government concerns about artificial pesticides and a directive to label conventionally produced foods with the pesticides used in their production – a move fiercely resisted by the agrochemical industry. We can expect to see more organic farms like Fairview Gardens in southern California, which has five hectares (12 acres) of land and is surrounded by a city. The land has been carefully nurtured into producing a variety of organic crops. In a good year, they harvest over 13,500kg (30,000lb) of peaches, plums and citrus fruit, and tons of fresh vegetables, avocados, berries and herbs for the local population.

Worldwide the organic movement is growing and expanding. Having adopted an organic agriculture policy in 1990, Cuba took just six years to become self-sufficient in basic fruit and vegetables. The use of artificial pesticides and nitrate fertilizers has been dramatically reduced and biological means are used to control around 80 per cent of pests. In Peru, terraces cut into the steep slopes of the Andes are still producing crops of organic beans and barley for Peruvian farmers today, as they did for their Inca ancestors.

Europe is a special case. Here, organic farming varies widely. In Italy there are some 36,600 organic farms, which produce everything from olives to oranges. Small farmers' co-operatives, whose products include organic pasta, olive oil, vinegar and wines, were set up around 30 years ago. Sweden, which in 2000 has cut artificial pesticide use to

Organic farming is practised *worldwide* and

25 per cent of what it was in 1987 and has banned 37 artificial pesticides because of the damage they cause to health or the environment, has 3,400 organic farms. In Germany, the babyfood industry is largely organic.

In the UK 3.7% of the utilisable agricultural area (UAA) is organic. The percentage land area farmed organically is marginally higher than the European average, but remains lower than in Sweden, Austria, Italy, Denmark and Finland.

In other parts of the European Union (EU) the governments of several countries, including France and the Netherlands, have adopted action plans and targets for encouraging the conversion from conventional to organic farming. In the UK, this change has been left to market forces, which will always slow down conversion. A conventional farmer moving to organic has to endure a two-year conversion period during which time yields will drop because artificial pesticides and antibiotics are not used, yet higher prices cannot be obtained because the produce is not fully organic. Twelve of the EU member countries provide organic farmers with maintenance payments after the conversion programme. Only three countries, including the UK, do not. Despite this, organic food consumption in the UK continues to grow by over 30 per cent a year, an amazing statistic considering that most of this demand has to be met by importing foods.

Production of organic food is increasing rapidly in Latin America and the Pacific region, particularly in Mexico, Australia and New Zealand. If this trend continues, and it seems certain to, we can look forward to more food being produced to organic standards.

THE RISING POPULARITY OF ORGANIC FOOD

The following statistics illustrate the explosion in popularity of organic food around Europe:

• Sales of organic fruit and vegetables are increasing by 30% a year, but today as little as 3.7% of the utilisable agricultural area in the UK is farmed organically

• Organic produce accounts for around 10% of the market in Germany, Switzerland, Austria, Denmark, Finland and Sweden; around Europe the average is about 2.5%

• Retail sales from organic food in Germany are worth a staggering £2.3 billion.

is well *established* in many countries

RECIPES

The pleasure of feeding your child and being appreciated for your efforts cannot be underestimated. These recipes have been created to offer a variety of flavours and textures using simple and tasty organic ingredients.

4~7 months

MOVING ON FROM MILK FEEDS

BREAST OR FORMULA MILK IS THE ONLY SUITABLE FOOD DURING THE FIRST FOUR TO SIX MONTHS. AFTER THIS, YOUR BABY NEEDS SOME SOLID FOOD IN HER DIET.

Weaning normally starts between four and six months because a baby's tiny digestive system is not fully developed until this age. Until then, breast or formula milk gives your baby all the nutrients he needs. The government advises that weaning should not begin until six months and the very earliest must be 17 weeks from birth. Before this time, a baby is unable to digest complex new foods and health problems may result. For this reason, I believe that when it comes to weaning, the later the better!

First foods *for* your baby

The basics of weaning

Between four and seven months of age your baby starts to show that she is ready for solids. Many babies can sit with help, hold food in their mouths and mix it with saliva. They may chew anything within reach, drool or cry when they see food and appear hungry after milk feeds.

Once you have decided to start weaning, you can establish a regular mealtime when you give your baby your undivided attention. Some babies are hungriest in the morning, others in the evening.

Initially, try offering your baby small amounts of food on the end of a spoon. Some babies eat what is offered and look around for more. Others may protest at a spoon being placed in their mouths. The majority swallow some food and dribble the rest down their chins. Each day, offer your baby extra teaspoonfuls of food if she seems hungry. About two weeks after the first meal, introduce a second. If feeding progresses well, offer a third meal after two more weeks.

Preparing purées

For the first food, try mixing boiled rice with water, formula or breast milk and puréeing it to the consistency of thick soup. Alternatively, try a pure baby rice. If this is well received, try introducing cooked, puréed apple or pear. For a third meal, try cooked, puréed potato or carrot.

An increasing number of puréed organic fruit and vegetables are produced commercially for babies. However, it is easy to make your own purées. Some foods, such as banana, can be simply mashed with a fork.

Always try to buy certified organic ingredients, particularly for these essential first foods.

Organic superfoods

RICE Rice is rich in protein and B vitamins and is gluten-free. Organic rice is grown without artificial pesticides.

BREAST MILK The ultimate superfood, breast milk is produced to satisfy your baby's specific needs.

Other foods can be pushed through a sieve, but a hand blender or food processor is a time-saving purchase. Fibres and pips should be removed and fruit and vegetables should be peeled before cooking and puréeing. At this age, very fibrous matter is difficult for a baby to digest.

You should start to add more protein – meat, fish, cheese, yoghurt and beans – to your baby's diet. Protein should be introduced gradually, at first just once a day, to avoid straining your baby's kidneys.

Weaning around the world

In every culture, weaning aims to accustom babies to the staple diet, while relying on milk as the main source of nutrition. In countries where food is in short supply, mothers may breast-feed for up to two years.

Weaning foods are universally bland and of high carbohydrate composition. In many cases, recipes for traditional weaning foods have been passed down through generations. In Asian countries, rice is the basis of kedgeree or kongi, which is fed to babies from five months of age. Initially, boiled, sieved rice is added to cooked lentil juice. As babies mature, puréed lentil is added to rice; followed by peas, carrots, tomato pulp, dill, coriander and sometimes yoghurt. Kongi, in China, is supplemented with vegetables, fish or chicken. In the Caribbean, first foods are often steamed. For example, steamed white fish and pumpkin are puréed with cho-cho, a local vegetable. Parents also offer their babies puréed chicken casserole or fish. In Africa, maize porridge or rice forms the first food, to which vegetable and protein-rich foods are gradually added. In Mexico and much of South America, first foods are based on potatoes, corn, peppers, beans and tortillas.

Q&A

WHY DOES MY BABY CRY AND REFUSE FOOD EVEN THOUGH I AM SURE SHE IS HUNGRY?

Your baby may not enjoy her first taste of solid food if she is very hungry. Before offering the first meal, give a short milk feed first.

I AM RETURNING TO WORK. SHALL I SWITCH FROM BREAST TO FORMULA MILK?

This is not a good time because you are asking your baby to cope with two big changes: your absence and feeding from a bottle. It is best to make a transition from breast milk to formula milk either a couple of weeks before or after you start work.

The early weeks of weaning are a time to encourage your child to try new **TEXTURES** and **TASTES**. Here I've taken my favourite simple **VEGETABLES** and made a nutritious **BRIGHT YELLOW PURÉE**.

Baby's First Vegetables

1 tsp olive oil

1 large carrot, peeled and chopped

1 potato, peeled and chopped

1 tbsp peas, fresh or frozen

2 tbsp sweetcorn kernels, frozen or tinned (unsalted)

4 tbsp water

Heat the olive oil in a small pan over medium heat. Add the carrot and fry until soft, about 5 minutes.

Add the potato, peas, sweetcorn and water and stir to mix. Bring to the boil, then reduce the heat, cover and simmer for about 15 minutes, stirring occasionally to prevent sticking.

Purée by pushing through a sieve or by using a liquidizer. Add a little more water if a thinner consistency is preferred.

makes	suitable for	storage	preparation	nutritional value
2–3 servings for a 4-month-old; 1 serving for a 6-month-old	vegetarians; those intolerant to gluten, milk and lactose	24 hours in the refrigerator; 4 weeks in the freezer	15 minutes + 20 minutes cooking time	Good source of ★ complex carbohydrates ★ vitamin E

Babies need high-energy foods because they grow so rapidly. This recipe contains a tasty organic olive oil to boost its energy level.

ORGANIC APPLES are often grown from traditional varieties such as Worcester Permaines and Coxes. They tend to be more resistant to pests so farmers can **AVOID** the use of artificial **PESTICIDES** and fungicides.

Apple and Apricot Purée

2 small eating apples, peeled, cored and finely chopped

2 peeled fresh apricots or 6 dried apricots, finely chopped

Place the apples and apricots in a pan and just cover with water.

Bring to the boil, then reduce the heat, cover and simmer for about 5 minutes. Strain the water and keep to one side.

Purée the fruit mixture by pushing through a sieve or by using a liquidizer. Add a little of the reserved water if a thinner consistency is preferred.

makes	suitable for	storage	preparation	nutritional value
2–3 servings for a 4-month-old; 1 serving for a 6-month-old	vegetarians; those intolerant to gluten, milk and lactose	24 hours in the refrigerator; 4 weeks in the freezer	10 minutes + 10 minutes cooking time	Good source of ★ vitamin A

The fresh taste of apples and apricots combined in a soft purée makes this an ideal dessert after a savoury lunch.

Fruit Compote - Baby's First Christmas

75ml (2½fl oz) water

½ tbsp oats

½ small eating apple, peeled, cored and finely chopped

1 peeled fresh apricot or 4 dried apricots, finely chopped

½ dried fig, chopped

pinch cinnamon

2 tsp sultanas

Place all the ingredients in a small pan and bring to a boil over high heat. Reduce the heat, then cover and simmer for about 5 minutes, stirring occasionally to prevent sticking.

Purée the fruit mixture by pushing through a sieve or by using a liquidizer. Add a little more water if a thinner consistency is preferred.

This is a version of **CHRISTMAS PUDDING** but without the fat and sugar of the traditional dish. Babies love it, so I also make it at other times of year – when I call it **FRUIT COMPOTE**.

makes	suitable for	storage	preparation	nutritional value
2–3 servings for a 4-month-old; 1 serving for a 6-month-old	vegetarians; those intolerant to milk and lactose	24 hours in the refrigerator; 4 weeks in the freezer	10 minutes + 5–10 minutes cooking time	Good source of ★ iron ★ vitamin C

Babies enjoy the taste and sensation of very small amounts of spices and herbs in their food – babyfood should not be bland.

BERRIES add a tang to sweeter dishes and are rich in **VITAMIN C** and many **MINERALS**. This simple recipe combines the smooth texture of mashed **BANANAS** with the high **ENERGY** content of **RICE**.

Banana and Berries

4 tbsp water

½ tbsp baby rice or ground rice

1 banana, finely chopped

10 berries such as raspberries, strawberries or blueberries, in any combination, fresh or frozen

Bring the water to the boil in a small pan. Add the remaining ingredients and simmer gently for about 5 minutes, stirring occasionally to prevent sticking.

Purée the fruit mixture by pushing through a sieve or by using a liquidizer. Add a little more water if a thinner consistency is preferred.

makes	suitable for	storage	preparation	nutritional value
2–3 servings for a 4-month-old; 1 serving for a 6-month-old	vegetarians; those intolerant to gluten, milk and lactose	24 hours in the refrigerator; 4 weeks in the freezer	5 minutes + 10 minutes cooking time	Good source of ★ iron ★ vitamin C

Try to use berries that have been harvested when they are in season – their nutrient levels will be much higher.

Mothers have relied on prunes over the years as a great natural aid to relieving constipation in a baby.

Fruity Porridges

BANANA PORRIDGE

½ tbsp oats

150ml (5fl oz) water

1 small, ripe banana, mashed

2 tsp sultanas

PRUNE AND APPLE PORRIDGE

½ tbsp oats

150ml (5fl oz) water

1 small eating apple, peeled, cored and chopped

4 dried prunes, finely chopped

APRICOT PORRIDGE

½ tbsp of oats

150ml (5fl oz) water

2 small, peeled, fresh apricots or 5 dried apricots, finely chopped

½ tbsp sultanas

Put all the ingredients in a small pan, cover and bring to the boil.

Reduce the heat and simmer gently for about 5 minutes, stirring occasionally to prevent sticking.

Purée by pushing through a sieve or by using a liquidizer. Add more water if a thinner consistency is preferred.

makes 2–3 servings for a 4-month-old; 1 serving for a 7-month-old
suitable for vegetarians; those intolerant to milk and lactose
storage 24 hours in the refrigerator; 4 weeks in the freezer
preparation 10 minutes + 6 minutes cooking time
nutritional value Good source of ★ B vitamins

Always try to buy organic bananas – there is a real difference in the way they are grown and, I believe, in the way they taste.

This recipe is a gentle introduction to **DAIRY** products – the cheddar cheese is just enough to give the dish a **CHEESY** flavour, without being too overpowering for your baby's palate.

Potato and Cheese Dinner

1 tsp olive oil

½ small onion, chopped

1 potato, peeled and chopped

2 tbsp milk

3 tbsp water

1 tbsp grated cheddar cheese

Heat the olive oil in a small pan over medium heat. Fry the onion until soft, about 5 minutes. Add the potato and heat gently for 1 minute.

Add the milk and water and stir to mix. Cover and simmer, stirring occasionally to prevent sticking, until the potatoes are soft, about 15 minutes. Remove from the heat and stir in the cheese until melted.

Purée by pushing through a sieve or by using a liquidizer. Add more water if a thinner consistency is preferred.

makes	suitable for	storage	preparation	nutritional value
2–3 servings for a 4-month-old; 1 serving for a 6-month-old	vegetarians; those intolerant to gluten	24 hours in the refrigerator; 4 weeks in the freezer	15 minutes + 20 minutes cooking time	Good source of ★ calcium

Avoid adding salt to a young baby's food, and be cautious about using naturally salty foods such as cheese or smoked fish.

Tomato and Chicken Casserole

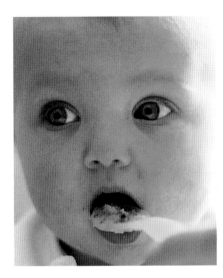

My **MOTHER**, Betty, used to make a wonderful chicken casserole for me and my sister when we were children – this is my memory of that dish, made suitable for a young **BABY**.

1 tsp olive oil

1 small onion, chopped

1 carrot, peeled and chopped

pinch ground oregano

1 small potato, peeled and chopped

2 tsp peas, fresh or frozen

1 tbsp chopped chicken breast or thigh meat, raw or cooked

2 tsp tomato purée

1 tbsp haricot or butter beans, tinned or boiled (unsalted)

5 tbsp water

Heat the olive oil in a small pan over medium heat. Fry the onion, carrot and oregano until soft, about 5 minutes.

Add the potato, peas, chicken, tomato purée, beans and water and stir to mix. Cover and simmer for about 20 minutes.

Purée by pushing through a sieve or by using a liquidizer. Add more water if a thinner consistency is preferred.

makes	suitable for	storage	preparation	nutritional value
2–3 servings for a 4-month-old; 1 serving for a 6-month-old	those intolerant to gluten, milk and lactose	24 hours in the refrigerator; 4 weeks in the freezer	15 minutes + 20 minutes cooking time	Good source of ★ iron

Non-organic chickens are often fed with such a lot of antibiotics that they are best avoided when cooking for your baby.

RATATOUILLE, with its soft **MEDITERRANEAN VEGETABLES**, is a lovely meal for a baby. This is a version with added chicken and root vegetables to **BOOST PROTEIN** and **ENERGY LEVELS.**

Mediterranean Vegetables and Chicken

1 tsp olive oil

1 small onion, chopped

1 large carrot, peeled and chopped

¼ courgette, peeled and chopped

1 mushroom, chopped

1 small strip red pepper, chopped

pinch finely chopped fresh rosemary

1 plum tomato, skinned, seeded, if desired (see below), and chopped, or 2 tsp tomato purée

1 potato, peeled and chopped

1 tbsp chopped chicken breast or thigh meat

2 tsp peas, fresh or frozen

125ml (4fl oz) water

Heat the olive oil in a small pan over medium heat. Add the onion, carrot, courgette, mushroom, red pepper and rosemary and fry until soft, about 5 minutes.

Meanwhile, if using a plum tomato, skin and seed it: place the tomato in a heat-proof bowl, pour over boiling water to cover and leave to stand for 1 minute. Drain, then pour over cold water to cover. Drain again, then use a sharp knife to peel away the skin. To seed, cut into quarters and simply scrape away the seeds.

Add the tomato or tomato purée, potato, chicken, peas and water to the fried vegetables. Bring to the boil, then reduce the heat, cover and simmer for about 20 minutes, stirring from time to time.

Purée by pushing through a sieve or by using a liquidizer. For a thinner consistency, add a little more water.

makes	suitable for	storage	preparation	nutritional value
3–4 servings for a 4-month-old; 2 servings for a 6-month-old	those intolerant to gluten, milk and lactose	24 hours in the refrigerator; 4 weeks in the freezer	15 minutes + 25 minutes cooking time	Good source of ★ iron

Vary this recipe by using fresh, seasonal vegetables. These will not have travelled so far to reach your plate.

7~10 months

NEW TEXTURES AND FLAVOURS

BY SEVEN MONTHS OF AGE YOUR BABY CAN TRANSFER PIECES OF FOOD FROM HIS HAND TO HIS MOUTH, AND MAY TRY TO USE A SPOON.

Many babies now have their first teeth and can cope with lumpier foods. For example, fruit and vegetables can be mashed rather than puréed, and stringier foods such as beetroot can be introduced. If your baby can manage these consistencies, you can try feeding him organic meat, fish, poultry, beans and pulses. Now is also the time to introduce foods such as tiny pasta shapes, which will encourage chewing. Your baby may also begin to enjoy finger foods such as sticks of organic carrot or celery, fingers of toast or organic baby breadsticks.

An adventure *in* eating

DIET ESSENTIALS

Babies are born with a store of iron, which is topped up with iron from breast or formula milk. But by the age of 6 months, these stores start to run low, and unless babies are offered an iron-rich diet, they can become anaemic, which can delay growth and development.

• Haem iron. This form of iron is most easily absorbed by your baby's digestive system and is present in red meat, poultry, liver and oily fish.

• Non-haem iron. The vegetarian choice, non-haem iron is found in broccoli, spinach, watercress, prunes, apricots, peas, beans and lentils. Non-haem iron is most easily absorbed when eaten with vitamin C-rich foods, such as orange juice or green vegetables.

Emerging skills and independence

At seven months of age your baby is likely to be visually alert, active, mobile and able to transfer objects from hand to hand and from hand to mouth. He can probably roll from his back to his tummy, lift his head, sit with support and stand while being held. He sleeps less during the day and is ready for new experiences including the taste of new textured foods and feeding himself.

By encouraging your baby to hold a spoon or a piece of food, you encourage independence and help to develop co-ordination. You can encourage communication skills by discussing your baby's food with him. By maintaining eye contact, smiling, saying "yum, yum" and playing games, you can establish meal-times as happy times.

All babies are different – some eat whatever is put in front of them, others seem able to survive on next to nothing, which can make feeding time very stressful. If so, ask yourself if your baby really needs a certain type or quantity of food. After all, this new eating adventure is not only about nutrition, it is also about your baby's emerging independence and his ability to make choices about the food he likes and dislikes.

A range of new experiences

First 'finger foods' could include a stick of organic carrot, a finger of toast or a breadstick. At this stage, your baby just sucks on the food. However, as he becomes more active his appetite will increase. He watches other people eating and drinking, and wants to copy them.

By 7 months of age babies need to eat an iron-rich diet to prevent them from becoming anaemic.

Many babies now have their first teeth and can cope with lumpier foods. For example, apple can be grated rather than steamed and puréed. If your baby can manage these consistencies, then stringier vegetables, such as carrots, can be mashed too. This is the time to try foods such as organic fish, meat and poultry. Make sure that you introduce meat – or pulses, such as beans and lentils – gradually.

Red meat should be offered to a non-vegetarian baby at least once a week. It is the richest and most efficiently absorbed source of iron. At first, try offering stock, for example with mashed vegetables. Once your baby is able to chew lumpier foods, you can incorporate minced meat.

Dried pulses and beans, also rich in iron, are popular with babies because of their smooth texture. Do cook them thoroughly as undercooked pulses can be difficult for a baby to digest. Red and brown lentils, chickpeas, black eye beans, haricot, flageolet and kidney beans are rich in carbohydrate, fibre, B vitamins, minerals, folic acid, selenium, iron and zinc. Buy organic as residues can be present in non-organic varieties. Tins of organic baked beans, with no added sugar or salt, are also available and make excellent storecupboard standbys.

New chewing skills mean that your baby can try cereals such as organic oat porridge accompanied by fresh puréed fruit. Or try pasta – a great food that encourages babies to chew and use their jaw muscles.

All the time that your baby continues to master eating solid food, breast or formula milk remains the most nutritionally important food. Health experts recommend that cow's milk should not yet be offered as a drink. However, it is fine in cooked foods such as cauliflower cheese or rice pudding. Organic yoghurts may also be added to puréed fruit.

Q&A

HOW MUCH MILK SHOULD I GIVE TO MY 7-MONTH OLD BABY?

Once your baby has established a pattern of eating, offer breast or formula milk as an after-meal drink only. This is particularly important at breakfast time. Giving food first not only encourages good eating habits, but after a night's sleep may form the largest meal. As your baby gets older he will reduce his own milk intake as his food intake increases.

WHAT TYPE OF WATER SHOULD MY BABY DRINK?

Offer either cooled, boiled tap water or sterilized, bottled water. Mineral water is not suitable for babies.

Organic superfoods

BANANAS A high-energy food that is easily digested, bananas are a rich source of vitamins B and C, potassium, magnesium and iodine.

MEAT This provides the perfect combination of iron and zinc. Beef and lamb are richest in iron, followed by pork and chicken.

This makes a wholesome **BREAKFAST**, but it can be served at any time of day – babies love the **CREAMINESS OF OATS** and **FRUIT** mixed together.

Apple and Banana Breakfast

¾ tbsp oats

75ml (2½fl oz) water

1 small eating apple, peeled and finely chopped

½ small banana, mashed

½ tbsp chopped sultanas

Put the oats, water, apple and banana in a small pan and stir to mix. Bring to the boil, then reduce the heat, cover and simmer for 5–10 minutes.

Purée by pushing through a sieve or by using a liquidizer.

Add the sultanas, then set aside until cool and the sultanas are plump and soft.

makes
2 servings for a
7-month-old; 1 serving
for a 10-month-old

suitable for
vegetarians; those
intolerant to milk
and lactose

storage
24 hours in the
refrigerator; 4 weeks
in the freezer

preparation
10 minutes
+ 5–10 minutes
cooking time

nutritional value
Good source of
★ calcium

The more fruit the better – try adding berries when in season, or puréed tropical fruit for a tangy flavour.

Banana and Fig Porridge

3 tbsp water

½ tbsp oats

½ dried fig, finely chopped
or puréed

1 small banana, mashed

Put the oats and the water in a small pan and bring to the boil. Cover and simmer for about 5 minutes, stirring occasionally to prevent sticking.

Remove from the heat and stir in the fig.

Put the mixture to one side to cool, then add the banana and mix with a fork until well combined.

Figs add a **RICH, FRUITY TASTE** and **TEXTURE** to this recipe. Like prunes, when used carefully figs can also solve any lingering constipation as your baby adjusts from milk-only feeds.

makes	suitable for	storage	preparation	nutritional value
2 servings for a 7-month-old; 1 serving for a 10-month-old	vegetarians; those intolerant to milk and lactose	24 hours in the refrigerator; 4 weeks in the freezer	10 minutes + 5 minutes cooking time	Good source of ★ magnesium ★ vitamin C

Made with tomatoes, basil, parmesan cheese and a hint of garlic, this **TRADITIONAL PASTA SAUCE** is good served with small **PASTA SHAPES.**

Tomato and Basil Sauce with Pasta

1 tsp olive oil	½ small potato, peeled and chopped
½ very small onion, finely chopped	60g (2oz) tinned tomatoes, chopped
½ small celery stick, finely chopped	½ tsp cream cheese
½ small garlic clove, chopped	½ tsp grated parmesan
¼ tsp chopped fresh basil	3 tbsp water
1 small carrot, peeled and chopped	1 tbsp pasta shapes

Heat the oil in a small pan over medium heat. Fry the onion, celery, garlic and basil until soft, about 5 minutes. Reserve 1 tablespoon of the mixture. Add the carrot, potato, tomatoes, cream cheese, parmesan and water to the pan. Cover and simmer for 10 minutes.

Cook the pasta according to the directions on the packet and drain well. Purée or mash the sauce to a slightly lumpy texture. Stir in the reserved fried vegetables and extra water if a thinner consistency is preferred.

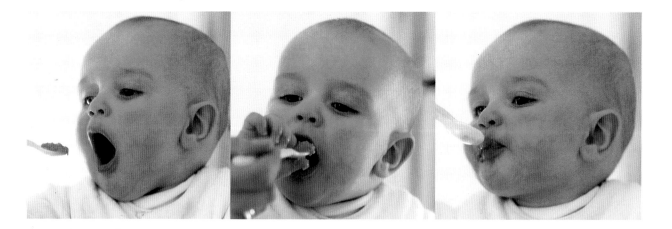

makes	suitable for	storage	preparation	nutritional value
2 servings for a 7-month-old; 1 serving for a 10-month-old	vegetarians; those intolerant to gluten	24 hours in the refrigerator; 4 weeks in the freezer	15 minutes + 15 minutes cooking time	Good source of ★ B vitamins ★ iron

You may think that this sauce will be too strong for your child, but it is a great favourite served with the milder flavour of pasta.

Bolognese Sauce with Pasta

½ tbsp olive oil

1 small onion, finely chopped

½ celery stick, finely chopped

1 small carrot, peeled and chopped

125g (4oz) finely minced beef

3 tomatoes, choppped, or 200g (7oz) tinned chopped tomatoes

90ml (3fl oz) water

1 tbsp fresh or frozen peas

pinch dried basil

1 tbsp pasta shapes

Heat the oil in a small pan over medium heat. Fry the onion, celery and carrot for about 2 minutes, then add the minced beef and brown for about 2 minutes.

Add the tomatoes and the water and bring to the boil. Reduce the heat, cover and simmer for 20 minutes, stirring from time to time. Add the peas and basil and simmer for a further 5 minutes.

Meanwhile, cook the pasta according to the directions on the packet and drain well.

Purée or roughly mash the bolognese mixture. Add the drained pasta and mix well.

Add extra water if a thinner consistency is preferred.

This classic **PASTA SAUCE** is a wonderful way to introduce your baby to **RED MEAT,** an excellent source of dietary **IRON.**

makes
2 servings for a 7-month-old; 1 serving for a 10-month-old

suitable for
those intolerant to gluten, milk and lactose

storage
24 hours in the refrigerator; 4 weeks in the freezer

preparation
15 minutes + 40 minutes cooking time

nutritional value
Good source of ★ iron

Don't purée these pasta sauce recipes too much – this type of meal should encourage your baby to chew.

At about 7 months babies need to start using the muscles that help them to chew and speak. Eating **TINY**, soft pieces of **PASTA** helps them to do this – making pasta an **IDEAL FOOD** for this age group.

Tomato and Cheese Sauce with Pasta

1 tsp olive oil

½ small onion, finely chopped

1 small carrot, peeled and finely chopped

very small pinch ground parsley

1 bay leaf

125ml (4fl oz) sieved tinned tomatoes or passata

2 tbsp water

2 tsp grated cheddar cheese

1 tbsp small pasta shapes (stars, alphabets, etc.)

Heat the oil in a small pan over medium heat. Lightly fry the onion and carrot until soft, about 5 minutes. Set aside half of the mixture.

Add the parsley, bay leaf, tomatoes or passata and water. Cover and simmer for 10 minutes, stirring occasionally to prevent sticking. Remove from the heat, add the cheese and stir well.

In a separate pan, cook the pasta according to the directions on the packet and drain well.

Remove the bay leaf, then purée or roughly mash the tomato and cheese mixture. Add the drained pasta and reserved vegetable mixture and mix well.

Add extra water if a thinner consistency is preferred.

makes
2 servings for a 7-month-old; 1 serving for a 10-month-old

suitable for
vegetarians

storage
24 hours in the refrigerator; 4 weeks in the freezer

preparation
15 minutes + 20 minutes cooking time

nutritional value
Good source of
★ vitamin C
★ vitamin E

If the pieces of pasta are too big, you can always liquidize or mash them at first.

The creamy taste of **COCONUT** makes it a popular ingredient in babyfood. Here, I have tried to reproduce a smooth korma by blending coconut with **MILD SPICES**, root vegetables, beans and **TOMATO**.

Vegetable and Coconut Korma

1 tsp olive oil

½ small onion, chopped

1 small carrot, peeled and diced

pinch each of ground ginger, cumin, coriander and turmeric

2 tsp tomato purée

1 small potato, peeled and finely diced

1 tbsp beans such as haricot or butter beans, tinned or boiled (unsalted)

2 tsp desiccated coconut

90ml (3fl oz) water

Heat the oil in a small pan over medium heat. Lightly fry the onion and carrot until soft, about 5 minutes.

Add the spices and tomato purée and heat for 3 minutes, stirring continuously. Put half of the mixture in a bowl and set to one side.

Add the potato, beans, coconut and water to the pan. Bring to the boil, then reduce the heat, cover and simmer for about 15 minutes.

Purée roughly or mash. Mix in the reserved vegetables, adding extra water if a thinner consistency is preferred.

makes	**suitable for**	**storage**	**preparation**	**nutritional value**
2 servings for a 7-month-old; 1 serving for a 10-month-old	vegetarians; those intolerant to gluten, milk and lactose	24 hours in the refrigerator; 4 weeks in the freezer	10 minutes + 25 minutes cooking time	Good source of ★ iron ★ magnesium

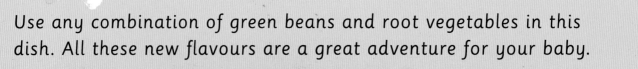

Use any combination of green beans and root vegetables in this dish. All these new flavours are a great adventure for your baby.

Sweetcorn and Potato

1 tsp olive oil

½ very small onion, finely chopped

1 small carrot, peeled and finely chopped

90ml (3fl oz) water

1 small potato, peeled and chopped

3 tbsp sweetcorn kernels from fresh or frozen cobs

½ tsp chopped fresh herbs such as basil, oregano or thyme

Heat the oil in a small pan over medium heat. Lightly fry the onion and carrot until soft, about 5 minutes. Put half of this mixture in a bowl and set to one side.

Add the water, potato and sweetcorn to the pan and stir to mix. Cover and simmer for about 15 minutes.

Add the herbs, then purée or roughly mash the mixture before adding the reserved vegetables. Add extra water if a thinner consistency is preferred.

Introduce your baby's eager taste buds to the new and **EXCITING FLAVOURS** of **SWEETCORN** and fresh **HERBS** with this simple **PURÉE**.

makes
2 servings for a
7-month-old; 1 serving
for a 10-month-old

suitable for
vegetarians; those
intolerant to gluten,
milk and lactose

storage
24 hours in the
refrigerator; 4 weeks
in the freezer

preparation
10 minutes
+ 20 minutes
cooking time

nutritional value
Good source of
★ complex
carbohydrates

This is a **DELICIOUS**

COMBINATION of

fruit with chicken

and rice – a

NUTRITIOUS BLEND

that I first saw fed

to babies in **NORTH**

AFRICA. This

version has fewer

SPICES and less

DRIED FRUIT.

Fruity Rice with Chicken and Apricot

1 tsp olive oil

½ small onion, chopped

1 small peeled fresh apricot, or 2 dried apricots, chopped

1 tbsp chicken breast or thigh meat, raw or cooked

1 plum tomato, skinned, seeded, if desired (see page 42) and chopped, or 2 tsp tomato purée

2 tsp sultanas

¼ tsp finely chopped fresh rosemary

pinch each ground coriander and cinnamon

¼ tsp finely chopped garlic

90ml (3fl oz) water

1 tbsp basmati rice

Heat the oil in a small pan over medium heat. Add the onion and fry until soft, about 2 minutes.

Mix in the apricot, chicken, tomato or tomato purée and sultanas.

Add the herbs, spices, garlic and water. Bring to the boil, then reduce the heat, cover and simmer for about 20 minutes, stirring occasionally to prevent sticking.

In a separate pan, boil the rice according to the packet instructions.

Add half of the cooked rice to the pan and reserve the rest.

Roughly purée or mash the fruity mixture, then add the reserved rice and mix well. If your child is not used to lumpy food, you may want to purée the whole meal in a liquidizer. Add extra water if a thinner consistency is preferred.

makes	suitable for	storage	preparation	nutritional value
2 servings for a 7-month-old; 1 serving for a 10-month-old	those intolerant to gluten, milk and lactose	24 hours in the refrigerator; 4 weeks in the freezer	15 minutes + 20 minutes cooking time	Good source of ★ calcium

Try serving this dish with couscous instead of rice – your baby may prefer the smaller grains.

Made with apple,

JUICY CHERRIES

and the sweetest

SEASONAL BERRIES,

this is a **DELICIOUS**

vitamin-rich dessert.

Berries and Cherries

75ml (2½ fl oz) water

1 tsp ground rice

1 tsp basmati rice

1 large eating apple, peeled, cored and finely chopped

4 raspberries

1–2 strawberries

2 cherries, stoned and chopped

Bring the water to the boil in a small pan. Add the ground and basmati rice, cover and simmer for about 10 minutes, stirring occasionally to prevent sticking.

Add the fruit and simmer until the apple is soft, about 10 minutes.

Purée by pushing through a sieve or by mashing the fruit with a fork. Add extra water if a thinner consistency is preferred.

makes	suitable for	storage	preparation	nutritional value
2 servings for a 7-month-old; 1 serving for a 10-month-old	vegetarians; those intolerant to gluten, milk and lactose	24 hours in the refrigerator; 4 weeks in the freezer	5 minutes + 20 minutes cooking time	Good source of ★ iron ★ vitamin C

Use any soft berries in this purée – seasonal ones will taste the best. Lightly cook the fruit to preserve its vitamin content.

In this **DELECTABLE** rice pudding, the fresh, tangy taste of **APRICOTS** is offset by the **SWEETER** flavour of **SULTANAS**.

Rice Pudding with Apricots

75ml (2½ fl oz) water

1 tbsp ground rice

1 tsp basmati or white short-grain rice

1–2 fresh apricots, peeled, or 6 dried apricots, finely chopped

1 tsp sultanas

2 tsp natural yoghurt

Bring the water to the boil in a small pan. Add the ground and basmati or short-grain rice and simmer gently for 5 minutes, stirring occasionally to prevent sticking.

Add the apricots and sultanas and simmer for about 5 minutes. Use a slotted spoon to set aside about a tablespoon of this mixture.

Purée the rest of the mixture by pushing through a sieve or by using a liquidizer. Stir in the reserved mixture, the yoghurt and water if a thinner consistency is preferred.

makes
2 servings for a 7-month-old; 1 serving for a 10-month-old

suitable for
vegetarians; those intolerant to gluten

storage
24 hours in the refrigerator; 4 weeks in the freezer

preparation
5 minutes
+ 10 minutes cooking time

nutritional value
Good source of
★ vitamin A

You can use any type of natural yoghurt, but wholemilk yoghurt is best for your child as it is the most energy-dense.

Banana and Mango Coulis

75ml (2½ fl oz) water

1 tbsp ground rice

½ juicy ripe mango

1 small banana

Bring the water to the boil in a small pan. Add the rice, cover and simmer very gently for about 5 minutes, stirring occasionally to prevent sticking. Remove from the heat and set aside to cool to just above room temperature.

Purée the mango and half of the banana in a liquidizer, or by pushing it through a sieve.

Combine the purée with the rice and serve with the remaining banana pieces.

Mangoes with their **VELVETY** flesh, rich yellow colour and distinctive **AROMATIC** smell are a **DELIGHT** for a baby. Organic mangoes will have been grown without artificial pesticides.

makes
2 servings for a
7-month-old; 1 serving
for a 10-month-old

suitable for
vegetarians; those
intolerant to gluten,
milk and lactose

storage
24 hours in the
refrigerator; 4 weeks
in the freezer

preparation
5 minutes
+ 20 minutes
cooking time

nutritional value
Good source of
★ vitamin C

10~15 months

HEALTHY MEALS AND SNACKS

THIS IS A TIME OF DISCOVERY, NEW SKILLS AND BEING ENCOURAGED BY YOU. THE KEY TO ALL THIS LEARNING IS PLAY – MUCH OF WHICH CAN HAPPEN AT MEAL-TIMES.

At around ten months your baby will be beginning to stand, holding on to the furniture or to you. He will soon stand alone and will take his first steps by about 15 months. He can now fit cubes into post boxes, place rings on a stick, throw a ball and build a small tower. By 15 months many babies can say single words, and some may produce two-word sentences. Some babies will still be breast-fed and some may be taking milk from a bottle. If you have not already done so, try introducing a cup.

Feeding *your* older baby

NEW FLAVOURS

Herbs have nutritional and therapeutic properties as well as enhancing the taste of food. Introducing them into your child's diet now encourages a love of variety and emphasizes that 'flavouring' should come from natural rather than heavily processed ingredients. Non-organic herbs are sometimes grown hydroponically (in a chemical solution with no soil), which means that they can have poor nutrient and essential oil levels. Buy organic herbs (see pages 140–41), and try growing some of the following at home, in the garden or in a window box:

• Parsley is very rich in vitamins A and C as well as iron, calcium and potassium

• Coriander is widely used in Asian weaning cuisine as it supplies essential oils beneficial to the digestive system

• Basil and oregano are rich in essential oils; basil is soothing and oregano can be invigorating.

Encouraging healthy snacking habits

Babies now have several teeth, which means that they can chew. Teeth brushing can be introduced as a game to be played each morning and evening, but it has a serious purpose – to establish the routine. You might want to find out about the fluoride status of the water in your area. As fluoride supplementation can be controversial, ask your doctor or dentist if you should choose a baby toothpaste with added fluoride.

You will be bombarded with snack foods for children, from biscuits and crisps to sweets and yoghurts, but while your baby is still too young to be influenced by peer pressure, you can encourage him to snack on fruit or simple savouries rather than sweets or heavily processed snacks. This helps to protect those precious first teeth and ensures that your baby gets the nutrition he needs. It also helps to develop a taste for healthier, less processed foods, which can become a lifetime habit.

Fruit and vegetables, rich in beta-carotene, flavenoids, vitamin C and potassium, make healthy snacks. However, non-organic produce may be treated with synthetic insecticides, herbicides and fungicides, or waxed to increase its shelf life. Tests by government agencies have found pesticide residues in a good share of non-organic fruits. Although organic fruits may not always look as good as the seemingly perfect non-organic fruits with shiny surfaces and blemish-free skin, they often taste so much better. You may have to pay a little extra, but seeking out the organic option is one way to be sure that you are giving the best to your baby.

Dried fruits or simple savoury biscuits are a good alternative to sweets and make a nutritious snack for your baby.

Organic superfoods

FISH Two portions of organic fish a week give your baby all the Omega 3 oil he needs.

DRIED FRUITS Dried apricots are a good source of carotene, potassium, iron and fibre. Prunes contain vitamin B6.

New foods to introduce

Fish is rich in Omega 3 oil, vital to brain and nervous tissue development. Indeed, Australian research has revealed that those in lower IQ brackets eat less oily fish than those in higher brackets. Fish such as sardines, mackerel and tuna contain other essential nutrients such as vitamins B and D, iron, zinc and iodine. Non-organic farmed fish has been found to contain traces of antibiotics and other residues.

Introduce some of the wide range of dried fruits available, including dates, figs, mango, pineapple, papaya and banana. However, unless they are organic they will have been treated with oils and preservatives and may also have been dipped in sugar and fried. One of the common treatments is to expose dried fruits to sulphur dioxide to preserve their colour. This can have detrimental effects on children, especially those prone to suffering from asthma. Organic alternatives are darker in colour than non-organic fruits, but this is a sign of their superiority.

Onions, garlic and leeks add lots of flavour to your baby's food. Onions are a rich source of vitamin C and spring onions are also a good source of iron. Garlic has been traditionally associated with developing resistance to infection. Leeks are full of vitamins A, C, folic acid and potassium. However, the onion family may be heavily sprayed: an average onion may receive one burst of insecticide, five of herbicides and two of fungicides. Onions may also be treated with a growth regulator and, when harvested, with a sprout suppressant, so choose organic every time.

Unprocessed oats can lower blood cholesterol, stabilize blood sugar and are rich in vitamins B and E, calcium, magnesium and silicon. Organic oats are grown without synthetic herbicides, insecticides and fungicides.

Q&A

MY BABY DOES NOT WEIGH AS MUCH AS SOME OF MY FRIENDS' CHILDREN. HOW DO I KNOW IF HE IS GROWING NORMALLY?

It is not a good idea to compare your child with others. Take more notice of the growth chart your health visitor can plot for you which will show your baby's real progress.

MY BABY IS EASILY DISTRACTED WHEN I'M TRYING TO FEED HIM OR TEACH HIM SOMETHING. IS SOMETHING WRONG?

Only a tiny minority of children suffer from conditions such as hyperactivity and attention-deficit disorder, and these symptoms can sometimes be alleviated by changes to the diet. Your health visitor will be able to advise you.

Breakfast Surprise

2 tbsp oats

3 tbsp each of milk and water

1 tbsp natural yoghurt

75g (2½ oz) sultanas or other dried fruit, finely chopped

1 small eating apple

This is a version of the original Bircher Benner Swiss Muesli omitting the nuts and using **OATS** instead of wheat flakes. The use of natural **YOGHURT** adds to its nutrient value and aids the digestive process.

Combine all of the ingredients, except the apple, in a bowl, cover and store in the refrigerator overnight.

Before serving, grate the apple and stir into the oat mixture.

Serve cold in the summer, or heat gently for a warming winter breakfast.

makes
2 large servings for
a 15-month-old or
1 adult serving

suitable for
vegetarians

storage
24 hours in
the refrigerator

preparation
5 minutes + overnight
refrigeration

nutritional value
Good source of
★ calcium
★ vitamin D

Add mashed, fresh berries or diced, fresh peaches to make this a sunny, summer breakfast.

Mixed Fruit Compote

60g (2oz) strawberries, chopped

60g (2oz) raspberries

2 dried apricots, finely chopped

1 dried prune or fig, finely chopped

1 peach or nectarine, stoned and chopped

1 kiwi fruit, chopped

1 small eating apple or pear, cored and chopped

125ml (4fl oz) orange or grapefruit juice (unsweetened)

pinch ground ginger

Place the prepared fruit in a large bowl, and stir to mix. In a separate bowl, mix together the fruit juice and ginger. Pour the mixture over the fruit, stir and leave to stand for a few minutes to help the flavours blend.

Warm gently before serving or pour the compote into warm bowls.

A delicious way of eating **FRESH FRUIT**, this compote makes enough for all the family. The **SECRET** is in combining both soft and hard fruits in a citrus juice that is lifted lightly with a pinch of **GINGER**.

makes
8 servings for a
15-month-old or 2 child
and 2 adult servings

suitable for
vegetarians; those
intolerant to gluten,
milk and lactose

storage
eat immediately

preparation
10 minutes

nutritional value
Good source of
★ iron
★ vitamin C

If you cannot find **ORGANIC FISH**, try to buy **WILD** rather than farmed fish. Serve these fish cakes with green beans, halved tomatoes and a puréed root vegetable such as turnip.

Fishy Rissoles

500g (1lb) potatoes, cut into chunks

1 tbsp fresh lemon juice

30g (1oz) butter

200g (7oz) fresh white or pink fish such as cod or salmon, bones and skin removed, or 1 x 200g (7oz) tin salmon or tuna in oil or spring water, drained

milk for poaching

6 spring onions, trimmed and chopped

freshly ground black pepper

a little flour to prevent sticking

1 egg

2 tbsp milk

90g (3oz) fresh breadcrumbs

3 tbsp good quality vegetable oil

Cook the potatoes in a pan of boiling water until soft, about 12–15 minutes. Drain, and mash with the lemon juice and half of the butter.

If using fresh fish, poach it in a pan of milk: add enough milk to cover the fish, bring to the boil, then reduce the heat and simmer until the fish is no longer translucent, about 5–10 minutes. Drain the fish and chop into small pieces.

In a separate pan, fry the spring onions in the remaining butter until soft. Add the spring onions, fish and pepper to the potato mixture and combine. Divide the mixture into 8, and pat into burger shapes with floured hands.

Beat the egg and milk together in a bowl. Coat each burger first in the egg mixture, then in the breadcrumbs.

Heat half of the oil in a frying pan over medium heat, then turn the heat down to low and add 4 burgers. Fry, turning once, until golden brown, about 5 minutes on each side. Drain on kitchen towel and keep warm. Add the rest of the oil and repeat the process with the remaining burgers.

makes	suitable for	storage	preparation	nutritional value
8 rissoles	fish-eating vegetarians	freeze when cool and use within 1 week	25 minutes + 35 minutes cooking time	Good source of ★ B vitamins ★ vitamin D

You could ask your fishmonger to remove the fish bones and skin for you, and cut the fish into chunks.

Most young children like **PASTA** and **SAUCE**. With so many shapes available, from **MINI-ALPHABETS** to **ANIMALS**, it should be easy to find one that your child enjoys eating.

Creamy Mushroom Sauce with Pasta

1 tsp olive oil

½ small onion, finely chopped

6 small button mushrooms, finely chopped

½ small garlic clove, crushed

1 small potato, chopped

2 tbsp milk

3 tbsp water

1 tbsp small pasta shapes

1 tsp chopped fresh parsley

Heat the oil in a pan over medium heat. Fry the onion, mushrooms and garlic until soft, about 5 minutes. Reserve one-third of this mixture. Add the potato, milk and water to the pan and bring to the boil. Reduce the heat, cover and simmer for 10 minutes, stirring occasionally.

Cook the pasta according to the directions on the packet and drain well. Roughly purée the sauce in a liquidizer, or mash to a slightly lumpy texture with a fork. Add the reserved fried vegetables, parsley and more water if a thinner consistency is preferred.

makes
1 serving for a
15-month-old

suitable for
vegetarians

storage
24 hours in
the refrigerator

preparation
15 minutes

nutritional value
Good source of
★ vitamin C
★ vitamin E

Beef Casserole

2 tbsp good-quality vegetable oil

2 onions, sliced

1 tsp paprika

750g (1½ lb) stewing beef, cut into bite-sized pieces

30g (1oz) plain flour seasoned with salt and pepper

1 x 400g (13oz) tin chopped tomatoes

250g (8oz) potatoes, cut into chunks

250g (8oz) carrots, cut into chunks

150ml (¼ pint) water

125g (4oz) squash, pumpkin, aubergine or peas, optional

This can be cooked on the stove top or in the oven. If using the oven, preheat to 160°C, 325°F, Gas 3.

Heat the oil in a large pan over medium heat. Add the onions and fry until soft, about 5 minutes.

Add the paprika and stir-fry for 30 seconds. Toss the meat in the seasoned flour and add to the pan; stir for a few minutes while the meat browns.

Add the tomatoes, potatoes, carrots and water and bring to the boil. Reduce the heat, cover and simmer for 1½–2 hours either on the stove top or in a preheated oven.

Add the squash, pumpkin, aubergine or peas, if using, for the last 10–15 minutes of cooking.

This is a traditional casserole made with **BEEF, ROOT VEGETABLES** and **SPICES**. Serve with rice or noodles, or with baked potatoes and stir-fried shredded cabbage or sliced peppers.

makes
2 servings for a 15-month-old and 2 adult servings

suitable for
those intolerant to milk and lactose

storage
freeze when cool and use within 4 weeks

preparation
20 minutes
+ 1½–2 hours cooking time

nutritional value
Good source of
★ B vitamins
★ iron
★ vitamin A

Organic beef has a great flavour and will not have been treated with the growth stimulants used on conventionally reared animals.

Meatballs are popular with most children. They can be mixed with **CREAMY CHEESE**, **VEGETABLE** or **TOMATO SAUCES**. Here I keep it **SIMPLE** and serve them with a classic fresh tomato sauce.

Mini Meatballs in Herby Tomato Sauce

FOR MEATBALLS:

250g (8oz) lean minced pork, lamb or beef

½ small onion, finely chopped

60g (2oz) mushrooms, finely chopped

2 tsp finely chopped fresh herbs such as parsley or thyme

30g (1oz) fresh wholemeal breadcrumbs

1 egg yolk

1 tbsp good-quality vegetable oil

FOR TOMATO SAUCE:

250g (8oz) fresh tomatoes, skinned, seeded (see page 42) and chopped

150ml (¼ pint) water or vegetable stock

½ small onion, finely chopped

1 tbsp tomato purée

1 tbsp finely chopped fresh herbs such as basil, parsley or thyme

Preheat the oven to 180°C, 350°F, Gas 4.

For the meatballs, place all the ingredients, except the oil, in a bowl and mix thoroughly. Use your hands to divide and shape the mixture into 25 balls. Chill in the refrigerator while you make the sauce.

For the sauce, put all the ingredients in a pan and bring to the boil over medium heat. Reduce the heat, cover and simmer for about 15 minutes, stirring occasionally. Remove from the heat and leave to cool slightly, then liquidize.

Heat the oil in a frying pan over medium heat. Fry the meatballs, turning them frequently, until they are lightly browned all over, about 5–10 minutes. Put the meatballs in an ovenproof dish.

Pour the sauce over the meatballs, cover with a lid or foil and bake in the oven for about 45 minutes.

makes	suitable for	storage	preparation	nutritional value
25 small meatballs	those intolerant to milk and lactose	freeze when cool and use within 1 week	30 minutes + 45 minutes cooking time	Good source of ★ B vitamins ★ iron

You can introduce more texture by serving the meatballs with steamed or stir-fried crunchy vegetables.

PUMPKINS seem to be grown especially for children. They have such **FUNNY SHAPES** and **BRIGHT COLOURS** and look like abandoned **TOYS** in the fields at **HARVEST TIME**.

Pumpkin Stew-in-a-Pot

1 pumpkin or squash, about 3kg (6 lb)

3 tbsp good-quality vegetable oil

500g (1lb) minced pork or beef, or cooked unsalted beans such as haricot or butter beans

250g (8oz) onion, chopped

3 cooking apples, cored and cut into large chunks

125ml (4fl oz) water or stock

60g (2oz) raisins

1 tsp chopped fresh or ½ tsp dried basil or thyme

Preheat the oven to 180°C, 350°F, Gas 4.

Cut the top off the pumpkin or squash and discard. Cut the pumpkin or squash into quarters and scoop out and discard the seeds and stringy pulp. Place the pumpkin or squash pieces cut-side down in a large, deep baking dish with 1cm (½in) of water in the bottom. Cover with foil and bake in the oven until tender, about 2 hours.

Heat the oil in a pan and fry the meat or beans, onion and apple until tender, about 15 minutes. Add the remaining ingredients, cover and bring to a boil. Reduce the heat, then simmer for about 30 minutes, stirring occasionally to prevent sticking.

Drain the water from the pumpkin or squash. Use a spoon to scoop out the soft flesh, then discard the skin. Mix the flesh with the meat or bean mixture and return it to the baking dish. Cover with foil and return it to the oven until hot, about 20 minutes.

makes	**suitable for**	**storage**	**preparation**	**nutritional value**
4 servings for a 15-month-old	those intolerant to gluten, milk and lactose	best eaten on day of cooking	10 minutes + 2 hours 20 minutes cooking time	Good source of ★ B vitamins ★ iron ★ vitamin A

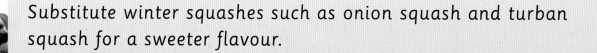

Substitute winter squashes such as onion squash and turban squash for a sweeter flavour.

Try baking sweet potatoes for a really delicious meal that will also be rich in beta-carotene.

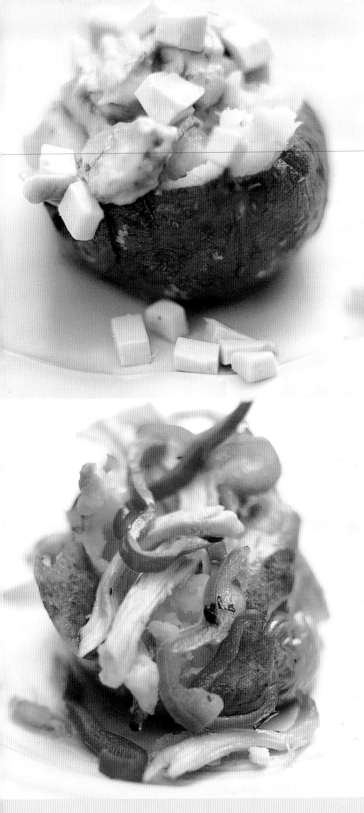

Jacket Potato Fillings

1 potato or sweet potato

FILLINGS

Hummus (see page 97)
and chopped apple

Avocado Dip (see page 78)

Vegetable and Coconut Korma (see page 54)

Dahl (see page 110)
with chopped tomato

Brussels sprouts,
tuna fish and
a little olive oil

Mashed boiled egg

Baked beans
and cream cheese

Diced or shredded chicken with sliced red
and green peppers and a little butter

Onion,
mushroom
and courgette fried in a little oil
with goat's cheese

Preheat the oven to 180°C, 350°F, Gas 4.

Prick the potato all over and bake in the oven
for 30–60 minutes, depending on the size of
the potato.

Serve with any filling – each one makes a
complete nutritionally balanced meal.

makes 1 serving per potato
suitable for check individual recipes; those intolerant to milk
and lactose should avoid cheese fillings
storage 24 hours in the refrigerator
preparation approximately 10–15 minutes, but check individual
recipes, + 30–60 minutes cooking time
nutritional value Potatoes are a good source of ★ vitamin B
★ vitamin C ★ potassium. Sweet potatoes are a good source of
★ vitamin C ★ vitamin E ★ magnesium

Cooking potatoes in their skins retains their high levels of
potassium and vitamins B and C.

Avocado's **RICH, CREAMY** texture makes it a great food for babies. Be sure to choose a soft, **RIPE** avocado for this recipe. Serve with lightly steamed sticks of carrot or courgette, or with strips of pitta bread.

Avocado Dip

½ ripe avocado

30g (1oz) cream cheese

1 tbsp finely chopped fresh plum tomato

2 tsp natural yoghurt

½ tsp finely chopped fresh mint or thyme

Blend all the ingredients in a liquidizer or mash together with a fork.

makes
1 serving for a
15-month-old

suitable for
vegetarians

storage
4 hours in the
refrigerator, but best
eaten immediately

preparation
5–10 minutes

nutritional value
Good source of
★ B vitamins
★ vitamin E

Blending avocado with cheese, yoghurt and tomato boosts the calcium and vitamin content of this dip.

Days Out Cakes

300ml (½ pint) natural yoghurt

30g (1oz) wholemeal flour

1 egg, beaten

½ tsp bicarbonate of soda

45g (1½oz) polenta (cornmeal)

a little butter or olive oil for frying

Mix together all the ingredients except the butter or olive oil in the order listed until the batter is smooth.

Lightly coat a frying pan with the butter or olive oil, and warm over medium heat. Drop a tablespoon of the batter into the pan and fry as though making pancakes. Fry until golden, about 2 minutes on the first side and a further minute on the second.

Transfer to a plate to cool, and repeat the process with the remaining batter.

These **NUTRITIOUS** cakes are based on a pancake recipe. I particularly like the use of **POLENTA,** which gives the cakes their **SPECIAL TEXTURE.** Spread them with cream cheese or fruit, and roll into wraps.

makes	suitable for	storage	preparation	nutritional value
10 cakes	vegetarians	2 days in the refrigerator; 4 weeks in the freezer	10 minutes + 20 minutes cooking time	Good source of ★ calcium ★ iron

These cakes make a good alternative to sandwiches and are much less messy to eat. Try them as a snack on car journeys.

Breadsticks

50g (8oz) strong bread flour
(brown or white)

1 tsp fast-action yeast

1 tsp sugar

150ml (¼ pint) warm water

2½ tsp salt

Measure the flour into a mixing bowl, add the remaining ingredients and mix until the dough is soft, smooth and comes away from the sides of the bowl.

Turn the dough onto a lightly floured work surface and knead for about 2 minutes, adding more flour, if necessary, to prevent sticking. Return it to the bowl, cover with a damp tea towel, plate or plastic wrap and leave to rise at room temperature until doubled in size, about 1 hour.

Preheat the oven to 190°C, 375°F, Gas 5.

Turn the dough onto the floured surface and knead for a few minutes, adding more flour, if necessary. Divide into 30 small plum-sized pieces. Roll each piece into a long, thin stick using your palms. Cut into smaller sticks, if desired. Place the sticks on a greased baking sheet and leave in a warm place for a further 20 minutes.

Bake in the oven for about 15–20 minutes. Cool on a baking rack.

WHOLESOME breadsticks are a **NATURAL** way to introduce your child to **FINGER FOODS** without the added sugar and flavourings of commercial rusks.

makes	suitable for	storage	preparation	nutritional value
30 x 18cm (7in) breadsticks	vegetarians; those intolerant to milk and lactose	1 week in an airtight container	10 minutes excluding waiting time + 20 minutes cooking time	Good source of ★ calcium ★ iron

For fruity breadsticks, add a handful of dried fruit such as currants, chopped apricots or figs to the dough at the first kneading.

BAKING BANANAS releases their full flavour and changes their texture to an **IRRESISTIBLE GOOEY PURÉE.** Serve with yoghurt, a drizzle of honey and flaked almonds if there is no history of nut allergy.

Baked Bananas

Whole, unpeeled bananas
(not green, but not too ripe) –
1 per person

Preheat the oven to 180°C, 350°F, Gas 4.

Place the bananas on a baking tray and bake for 25 minutes.

Remove from the oven. Allow to cool a little, then peel.

makes
1 serving per banana

suitable for
vegetarians; those
intolerant to gluten

storage
eat immediately

preparation
5 minutes
+ 25 minutes
cooking time

nutritional value
Good source of
★ vitamin C

Nuts are a nutritious addition to this recipe but must be used with care given the increasing incidence of nut allergies.

Toddler

INDEPENDENT FOOD CHOICES

BETWEEN 15 MONTHS AND TWO YEARS, YOUR BABY'S PHYSICAL, INTELLECTUAL, EMOTIONAL AND SOCIAL DEVELOPMENT BRING WELCOME INDEPENDENCE.

The average two-year-old can walk confidently, ride a tricycle, put on socks and complete jigsaws. By the age of two years, many children can articulate their needs and protests and can engage in dialogue. Remember that your toddler will copy what you do, not what you say. Between one and two years, she will interpret being offered family food as a sign that she is one of the family. The emotional and nutritional needs of toddlers cannot be separated.

Changing tastes *and* eating skills

CONVENIENCE FOODS

Convenience meals usually contain preservatives, additives, fillers and poor-quality fat or sugar which replace more nutritious ingredients. There are plenty of organic convenience foods:

• Pasta and sauce: children like the taste and texture of pasta, especially combined with their favourite sauce

• Milk: a pint of milk a day provides essential protein, fat, vitamins and minerals; supermarkets sell organic milk; give toddlers the full-fat variety to fuel their rapid growth; children who are lactose-intolerant can drink fortified soya milk

• Yoghurt: add chopped cucumber and mint, and serve with pitta bread for a delicious lunch; serve it with chopped fruit as an evening dessert

• Cheese: this is a popular finger food for toddlers; serve it on toast or baked potatoes.

A time of burgeoning independence

Your toddler experiences tumultuous emotional changes throughout her second year. There is good reason for this being known as The Terrible Two's. While on one hand your child has acquired new skills and independence, on the other hand she is still emotionally dependent on you. She is sometimes clingy and anxious if separated from you for any length of time.

This period of change is a challenge to parents. As your child becomes more independent you have to learn to release control and allow your developing toddler to make choices, learn from mistakes and understand that her actions have consequences. This is the well-recognized process of separation.

Nowhere is this more amply illustrated than in your toddler's changing food habits and eating skills. In many ways life was easy when your baby was in her highchair and you fed her with her food. An independent-minded toddler is free to leave the table and has clear opinions about likes and dislikes – which may seem to you to be completely without logic.

A strategic approach is needed to cope with this stage of your toddler's development. Decide what you will and will not encourage or tolerate, and set your own boundaries. This will help your child to develop greater confidence, and turn what could be a time of anxiety into a time of adventure and learning. A positive, encouraging environment produces a happy and confident toddler.

Why not let your toddler help you to bake delicious homemade bread.

Bread and potatoes

Rich in fibre, bread is a good source of iron, vitamins B and E and protein. In conventional bread the grains have been subjected to a range of artificial pesticides both during and after harvesting. During baking, flour improvers and a range of other preservatives may be added.

When choosing organic bread, look for a label that confirms that it has been certified organic. If you have difficulty finding a good loaf, you could try baking your own. Although time consuming, it can be fun if you get your child involved. Alternatively, invest in an inexpensive bread machine – they make delicious loaves, particularly if you add dried fruits, herbs, nuts, seeds or grated citrus zest. One final point – toddlers sometimes prefer simple white bread. Do not get into a battle if that is your child's choice; respect your child's wishes and try something new a month or two later.

Potatoes, a staple of the diet in many cultures, are highly nutritious. However, the non-organic varieties are repeatedly treated with artificial insecticides, herbicides and fungicides, as well as growth regulators, while they are in storage. They retain pesticide residues in their skins because they are in contact with them for longer while in the earth. For this reason, governments advise parents to peel non-organic root vegetables before serving them to children.

Q&A

WHAT SHOULD I DO WHEN MY TODDLER HAS A TANTRUM IN THE SHOP OVER A CHOCOLATE BAR?

Learn to negotiate. Don't say 'no,' and walk away, but don't give in for a quiet life. Distract your child by involving her in something else. Remind her that she can have a treat after lunch. Stay calm, despite feeling stressed.

SHOULD I INSIST THAT MY CHILD CLEARS HER PLATE?

It is more important to respect your toddler's appetite. This allows her to eat to satisfy her hunger and gives her a sense of autonomy. Praise her for the quantity eaten, and do not scold when food is unfinished.

Organic superfoods

POTATOES High in fibre and rich in vitamins B and C and potassium, as long as potatoes are organic, and therefore grown without pesticides, they are best cooked in their jackets for maximum nourishment.

BREAD A good source of iron, vitamins B and E and protein, bread is also rich in fibre. It is available in so many shapes and forms that you could introduce a new variety every day.

This recipe combines **ORANGES** with **APPLES,** creamy oats, yoghurt and **PLUMP SULTANAS** in my own version of a **HEALTHY** Swiss-style breakfast.

Apple and Orange Breakfast

freshly squeezed juice of 1½ oranges, or 4 tbsp unsweetened orange juice

½ tbsp oats

1 apple, cored and chopped

1 tsp natural yoghurt

small handful sultanas or raisins

Heat the orange juice and oats in a small pan and simmer for 5 minutes. Add the apple and simmer until soft, about 5 minutes.

Remove from the heat and stir in the yoghurt.

Add the sultanas or raisins and leave for a few minutes to plump up.

makes	suitable for	storage	preparation	nutritional value
1 child-sized serving	vegetarians	best eaten immediately	5 minutes + 10 minutes cooking time	Good source of ★ vitamin C

For a stronger orange flavour, add a tablespoon of grated orange zest to the oats while they are cooking.

Fruit Bread Fingers

60g (2oz) good-quality vegetable oil, butter or margarine

125g (4oz) runny honey

1 egg, beaten

125g (4oz) carrots or apples, grated

2 small bananas, mashed

90g (3oz) self-raising flour

60g (2oz) sultanas, dried cherries or cranberries

1 tsp lemon or orange zest, finely grated and chopped

Preheat the oven to 180°C, 350°F, Gas 4.

Cream the oil, butter or margarine with the honey in a mixing bowl. Gradually beat in the egg. Mix in the carrots or apples, bananas and flour; add the sultanas, cherries or cranberries and zest. Add a little extra flour, if necessary, until a spoon stands upright in the mixture.

Turn the mixture into a lightly greased 18cm (7in) shallow, square cake tin and level the surface. Bake until golden brown, about 45 minutes.

Cool slightly, then lightly mark into fingers using a sharp knife. Allow to cool completely in the tin, then cut into fingers to serve.

A tasty **FRUIT BREAD** makes an ideal quick **BREAKFAST** or a **SNACK** to beat hunger pangs. This one combines grated **APPLES** or **CARROTS** with **DRIED FRUIT** and **CITRUS ZEST.**

makes	suitable for	storage	preparation	nutritional value
10 fingers	vegetarians; those intolerant to milk and lactose	4 days in an airtight container; 1 week in the freezer	10 minutes + 45 minutes cooking time	Good source of ★ iron

These moist fruitcake fingers are tasty and nutritious and are sweetened naturally with honey, not sugar.

Butter beans make a **CREAMY, WHITE PURÉE** to which I add red vegetables for **TASTE** and **TEXTURE**. This is a warming dish for cold winter evenings and is delicious served with crusty bread and a salad.

Roasted Butter Bean Gratin

1 tsp good-quality vegetable oil

1 small leek, well washed and finely chopped

½ small carrot, grated

½ tsp crushed garlic

2 tbsp tinned or cooked butter beans, rinsed and drained

150ml (¼ pint) water or stock

1 tsp finely chopped fresh parsley, thyme or basil

¼ red pepper, finely chopped

1 tomato, cut into thin rings

60g (2oz) cheddar cheese, grated

30g (1oz) breadcrumbs

Preheat the oven to 180°C, 350°F, Gas 4.

Heat the oil in a pan over medium heat. Add the leek and carrot and fry gently for about 5 minutes. Add the garlic and butter beans and cook, stirring occasionally, for a further 5 minutes. Add the water or stock and herbs.

Purée the mixture in a liquidizer, then pour into an ovenproof dish and mix in the red pepper. Arrange the tomato rings on top. Mix the cheese with the breadcrumbs and sprinkle over the top. Bake in the oven until golden brown and bubbling hot, about 20 minutes.

makes	suitable for	storage	preparation	nutritional value
2 child-sized servings; 1 adult serving	vegetarians; those intolerant to gluten	24 hours in the refrigerator; 1 week in the freezer	15 minutes + 20 minutes cooking time	Good source of ★ iron

Try adding diced parsnip or turnip instead of carrot. Ground ginger works well either with, or instead of, the garlic.

Sausages with Mash and Gravy

2 good-quality sausages

FOR MASHED POTATO:

1 x 200g (7oz) potato, cut into chunks

1 tsp butter

2 tbsp milk

FOR GRAVY:

1 tsp olive oil

½ small onion, finely chopped

1 tsp cornflour

200ml (7fl oz) water

½ tsp tomato purée

Their easy-to-handle **SHAPE** and tasty **SEMI-SPICY** fillings make sausages an enduring **FAVOURITE** with children. Serve with mashed potatoes and **VEGETABLES** such as broccoli, peas and carrots.

Cook the sausages on a heated oiled griddle pan (or grill or barbecue) until browned all over and cooked through.

Meanwhile, make the mashed potato. Put the potato chunks into a pan of cold water, cover and bring to the boil. Reduce the heat and simmer until tender, about 10 minutes. Drain, add the butter and milk and mash until smooth.

Make the gravy: heat the olive oil in a small pan, add the onion and fry until translucent, about 3 minutes. Add the cornflour and stir to coat the onion. Add the water and tomato purée and bring to the boil, then reduce the heat and simmer for 5 minutes.

makes
2 child-sized servings

look for additive-free sausages with a high meat content

storage
cold cooked sausages can be kept for 24 hours in the refrigerator

preparation
15 minutes

nutritional value
Good source of
★ B vitamins
★ iron
★ zinc

Buy good quality and, if possible, organic sausages – cheap pork sausages use heavy flavourings to disguise poor-quality ingredients.

Lean **LAMB** is a **NUTRITIOUS** meat for young children and works very well with **ROOT VEGETABLES** and **SQUASH**. Serve this with steamed green vegetables such as **GREEN BEANS**, **BROCCOLI** or **MANGE TOUT** and rice, couscous or mashed potatoes.

Mediterranean Lamb

175g (6oz) lamb steaks, neck fillet or the meat in lamb chops, chopped

250g (8oz) pumpkin or squash, cubed

1 large carrot, chopped

½ tsp ground cinnamon

½ tsp ground cumin

1 tsp tomato purée

400g (13oz) fresh or tinned plum tomatoes

150ml (¼ pint) water

Preheat the oven to 160°C, 325°F, Gas 3.

Put all the ingredients in a casserole dish with a well-fitting lid. Cover and cook in the oven for 1 hour.

Remove from the oven and mash the vegetables into the gravy using a potato masher.

makes	suitable for	storage	preparation	nutritional value
3 child-sized servings	those intolerant to gluten, milk and lactose	24 hours in the refrigerator; 1 week in the freezer	10 minutes + 1 hour cooking time	Good source of ★ iron ★ vitamin A

This recipe is suitable for younger children if you process it in a liquidizer before serving.

Spicy Cheese and Potato Sticks

400g (13oz) mashed potato (see page 92 and double quantity)

125g (4oz) cheddar cheese, grated

½ tsp ground coriander

1 egg yolk, beaten

a little flour for dusting

a little beaten egg or milk for brushing

1 tbsp seeds such as fennel, caraway, sesame or sunflower, or a combination

A **GREAT SNACK** at any time of day, these potato sticks are a good way of introducing children to the complex **FLAVOURS** of **SPICES**. They make a tasty alternative to shop-bought snacks, which often include artificial flavourings.

Preheat the oven to 200°C, 400°F, Gas 6.

Mix the mashed potato, cheese, coriander and egg yolk in a bowl. Lightly flour a board or clean work surface. Roll out the potato mixture until about 2.5cm (1in) thick, then cut into finger lengths.

Brush the sticks with beaten egg or milk and roll in the seeds, gently pressing them into the potato to help them stick. Place them on a lightly oiled baking sheet and bake for 10 minutes until crispy and golden.

makes	suitable for	storage	preparation	nutritional value
10 sticks	vegetarians; those intolerant to gluten	24 hours in the refrigerator	15 minutes + 10 minutes cooking time	Good source of ★ calcium ★ iron ★ vitamin C

This is a great way to use up leftover mashed potato.

Fresh corn – from the greengrocer's, a box scheme or, better still, from the garden – is a true **SUPERFOOD**, rich in **NUTRIENTS** and delicious as well. Barbecued corn is fun to cook and to eat.

Barbecue Corn on the Cob

1 ear of corn per child, husk removed, cut in half
60g (2oz) butter, melted

Light the barbecue or preheat a gas barbecue.

Wrap each corn on the cob in foil, shiny side inwards.

Place the corn on the barbecue and cook for about 10 minutes, turning frequently with tongs.

Remove from heat, then unwrap and drizzle with melted butter.

makes	suitable for	storage	preparation	nutritional value
1 per child	vegetarians; those intolerant to gluten	eat immediately	5 minutes + 10 minutes cooking time	Good source of ★ B vitamins ★ magnesium

Take the corn out of the foil and let it cool before giving it to young children.

Hummus

400g (13oz) tinned chickpeas,
rinsed and drained, or 100g (3½ oz)
dried chickpeas, soaked overnight,
simmered for 60 minutes, drained

3 tbsp water

2 tbsp olive oil

freshly squeezed juice of ½ lemon

2 tsp tahini (optional)*

1 garlic clove, crushed

1 tsp chopped fresh parsley

Put the chickpeas and water in a food processor and liquidize until
the consistency of a smooth pâté.

Add the olive oil, lemon juice, tahini, if using, and garlic and process
to mix.

Transfer to a bowl and sprinkle with the parsley to serve.

* Omit the tahini if there is a history of nut allergies in the family.

Serve hummus as a **DIP** with pitta bread and **VEGETABLE FINGERS** or as a sandwich or jacket potato **FILLING**. It can also be served hot or cold as a **BABYFOOD PURÉE**.

makes	suitable for	storage	preparation	nutritional value
3 child-sized servings	vegetarians; those intolerant to gluten, milk and lactose	3 days in the refrigerator	5 minutes	Good source of ★ iron ★ vitamin C

*Traditional Middle-Eastern hummus contains tahini, or sesame
seed paste; add two teaspoons to boost iron levels.*

This **VIBRANT**, crunchy **SALAD** is packed with nutrients that will fortify the **IMMUNE SYSTEM** and promote **GOOD DIGESTION**. Serve with jacket potatoes and a protein-rich food such as dahl, **HUMMUS** or **CREAM CHEESE**.

Energy! Energy!

1 raw beetroot, grated

1 eating apple, grated

1 carrot, grated

60g (2oz) cabbage, finely sliced

30g (1oz) sunflower seeds

small handful dried fruit such as currants or dried cranberries

2 tsp olive oil

1 tbsp freshly squeezed lemon juice, or unsweetened orange juice

1 tsp runny honey

Combine the grated beetroot, apple, carrot and cabbage in a bowl. Mix in the sunflower seeds and dried fruit.

In a separate bowl, mix the olive oil, lemon or orange juice and honey together until well blended. Pour the mixture over the salad and toss until the salad is evenly coated.

makes 3 child-sized portions	**suitable for** vegetarians; those intolerant to gluten, milk and lactose	**storage** best eaten within 2 hours	**preparation** 10 minutes	**nutritional value** Good source of ★ vitamin A ★ vitamin C

Use red or white cabbage and hard fruits such as pears to vary tastes and textures in this salad.

This is a
MEDITERRANEAN
take on a traditional
British pudding.
It uses ingredients
widely used in Italian
cooking such as
CITRUS zest, olive
oil and **HERBS** and
is a firm **FAVOURITE**
with my family.

Italian Bread and Butter Pudding

4 large slices good-quality white or wholemeal bread, buttered on one side

30g (1oz) raisins, currants or cranberries, or other dried fruit such as cherries, prunes or figs, finely chopped

½ ripe apple or pear, cored and chopped into small pieces

2 eggs

30g (1oz) runny honey

1 tsp chopped fresh or ½ tsp dried sage, rosemary or thyme

grated zest of ½ lemon or small orange

½ tsp ground cinnamon

450ml (¾ pint) milk

drizzle of olive oil

Preheat the oven to 180°C, 350°F, Gas 4.

Cut the slices of bread into halves or quarters. Line the bottom of a greased ovenproof dish with one layer of bread, buttered side up. Sprinkle with a little dried fruit and apple or pear, cover with bread and continue the layering process.

Whisk the eggs, honey, herbs, zest, cinnamon and milk in a bowl and pour over the bread. Leave to stand for 30 minutes.

Drizzle over the olive oil and bake in the oven until golden, about 30 minutes.

makes		storage	preparation	nutritional value
2 child-sized servings and 2 adult servings	**suitable for** vegetarians	24 hours in the refrigerator; 1 week in the freezer	15 minutes + 30 minutes cooking time	Good source of ★ calcium ★ iron

Sage, rosemary or thyme work well in this recipe, but any dried herbs will do.

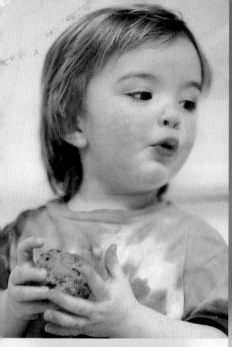

 Party food doesn't have to be unhealthy – children love fresh fruit and crunchy snacks such as breadsticks.

Fruity Birthday Cakelets

90g (3oz) butter

2 ripe bananas, mashed

1 egg, beaten

90ml (3fl oz) milk

1 tbsp runny honey

200g (7oz) self-raising flour

¼ tsp bicarbonate of soda

90g (3oz) sultanas

1 banana, sliced, for decorating

Preheat the oven to 200°C, 400°F, Gas 6.

Cream together the butter and banana in a bowl. Gradually work the egg, milk, honey, flour and bicarbonate of soda into the mixture. Stir in the sultanas. Divide the mixture between small paper cake cups.

Bake for 15 minutes in the middle of the oven until a skewer inserted into the middle of a cakelet comes out clean.

Remove from the oven and cool on a cake rack. Decorate with banana slices and candles.

FOR PEAR CAKELETS, follow the recipe above but substitute a mashed pear for one of the bananas and decorate with sliced pear pieces.

FOR STRAWBERRY CAKELETS, follow the recipe above but substitute four mashed strawberries for one of the bananas, and decorate with sliced strawberry or kiwi pieces.

makes 24 cakelets
suitable for vegetarians; those intolerant to milk and lactose
storage 4 days in an airtight container; 1 week in the freezer
preparation 15 minutes + 15 minutes baking time
nutritional value Good source of ★ vitamin B6 ★ vitamin C ★ magnesium ★ potassium

These festive cakelets are made without sugar and are decorated with fresh fruit.

Preschool

EXPLORING DIFFERENT FOODS

BETWEEN TWO AND FIVE YEARS CHILDREN BEGIN TO MOVE INTO SOCIETY, LEARNING TO BECOME MEMBERS OF MORE COMPLEX SOCIAL GROUPS.

By five years of age your child will be at school, eating meals in a range of locations, enjoying different foods and influenced in his tastes by the people with whom he comes into contact.

As a parent, you are faced with the challenge of meeting his nutritional needs in settings you do not control. Now that one in three people in the UK eat some organic food your child will not be unusual – an important factor, as children do not like being different. Organic bread, cheese, fruit and drinks in a lunch box can look exactly like their conventional counterparts.

Maintaining *a* balanced diet

The importance of breakfast

Breakfast is the first meal of the day after our longest fast. When
children wake up they need a quick burst of liquid, energy and protein
to give them the best start to their day. Porridge oats, bread or rice-
based cereals provide a complete package of complex carbohydrates,
vitamins, minerals and fibre that will be slowly released throughout
the morning. Add to that some organic fruit juice and fresh fruit.

Eggs can provide 20 per cent of the day's protein requirement
and contain potassium, iodine, folic acid, vitamin C and beta-carotene.
Children love French toast, omelettes and boiled egg with soldiers.
Free-range organic eggs are free from antibiotics, food additives and
other chemicals fed or injected into chickens. The birds are also reared
in conditions that show consideration for their natural instincts.

Vegetables and citrus fruit

Until recently, eating different vegetables clearly marked the seasons,
with root crops providing winter sustenance, and salads available only
in the summer. When you choose organic produce you resume this way
of eating because organic produce is not available in every form all year
round. Non-organic lettuce is always available because it is fed with
synthetic fertilizers and repeatedly sprayed.

By four years of age your child should be eating about 60g (2oz) of
vegetables each day – cooked, raw, frozen and tinned. Children usually
love raw vegetables such as carrots and celery. They are crunchy, sweet

**Research has shown that children who eat breakfast perform
significantly better at school than those who do not.**

Organic superfoods

GRAPES Packed with vitamin C, natural antioxidants and natural sugars, grapes give your child an instant energy boost.

CITRUS FRUIT Grapefruits and oranges are rich in beta-carotene, vitamin C, vitamins B1 and 6, potassium, folic acid, calcium and iron.

and make good finger foods – they are also extremely nutritious. Also try cucumber, which contains potassium and folic acid, as well as beta-carotene in the skin. Non-organic cucumbers should be peeled as they are waxed with a chemical wax to prolong their shelf-life.

Lettuce is rich in vitamins A and C, folic acid, potassium, calcium, and phosphorus. It also contains phytochemicals which naturally help to induce sleep. Organic lettuce can be obtained seasonally, and, unlike non-organic lettuce, none of the leaves need be discarded to avoid the worst of the pesticide residues. Non-organic produce may be sprayed with artificial pesticides, residues of which may affect the development of metabolic systems. For this reason you should always peel, top and tail non-organic produce before use. This will in some cases lessen residues, but because systemic chemicals may be used, conventional vegetables may contain residues. Organic vegetables just need a quick rinse.

Children can enjoy fruit if it is fun to eat. Kiwi fruits can be eaten like a boiled egg, with a spoon, and grapes make an ideal snack. Grapefruits or oranges, as fruit or juice, are an excellent way to wake up the palate after a long sleep. In 1998, residues were found in all 50 samples of non-organic oranges tested in the UK, so try to buy organic.

Q&A

HOW CAN I STOP MY CHILD FROM BECOMING OBESE?

Where possible, cook organic food, and keep convenience food for when you are really busy. Regard sweets as a rare treat; reward with love and time instead. Don't worry if your child leaves food – let him judge when he is full.

MY CHILD SUFFERS FROM CONSTIPATION. CAN YOU RECOMMEND A LAXATIVE?

Never give laxatives to young children – they cure the symptoms but not the problem. Avoid refined foods, and include more whole foods, fruit and vegetables in your child's diet.

Nutritious and **EASY TO PREPARE**, macaroni **CHEESE** is popular with most children. Here is a version with added **GOURMET** ingredients for a special treat.

Little Gourmet Macaroni Cheese

300ml (½ pint) milk

1 bay leaf

125g (4oz) small macaroni or pasta shapes

30g (1oz) butter

30g (1oz) cornflour or plain flour

60g (2oz) hard cheese such as cheddar, grated

1 small onion, finely chopped

60g (2oz) button mushrooms, finely chopped

60g (2oz) frozen peas

½ garlic clove, crushed

1 tsp finely chopped fresh herbs such as basil, sage or chives

Preheat the oven to 200°C, 400°F, Gas 6.

Heat the milk in a pan with the bay leaf. Bring to simmering point, then remove from the heat and set aside to cool.

Cook the pasta according to the directions on the packet and drain well.

In a separate pan, gently heat the butter. Add the flour and stir, using a wooden spoon or hand whisk, until well combined and smooth. Remove the bay leaf from the milk, then gradually add the milk to the pan, stirring continuously.

Stir the sauce over a medium heat until it begins to thicken. Simmer for 3 minutes, then stir in half the cheese, all the macaroni and the onion, mushrooms, peas, garlic and herbs.

Spoon into an ovenproof dish, sprinkle the remaining cheese over the top and bake for 20 minutes, until the top is bubbling and golden.

makes
4 child-sized servings

suitable for
vegetarians

storage
24 hours in the refrigerator; 1 week in the freezer

preparation
20 minutes
+ 20 minutes cooking time

nutritional value
Good source of
★ calcium
★ vitamin C

Any fresh, green herbs will enhance the flavour of a pasta sauce – use whatever you have to hand.

SPICY food can be very POPULAR with children, but be careful not to overdo it – very spicy food can put them off. Serve this with boiled RICE or a FLATBREAD such as naan or pitta bread for a perfectly balanced meal.

Dahl

1 tbsp good-quality vegetable oil

1 small onion, finely chopped

½ tsp turmeric

½ tsp ground coriander or cumin seeds

125g (4oz) red lentils, washed and picked over

1 carrot, finely chopped

300ml (½ pint) water

small handful shredded cabbage

Heat the oil in a pan over medium heat. Add the onion and fry gently until soft, about 5 minutes. Mix in the spices and cook for a further 2 minutes.

Add the lentils, carrot and water and bring to the boil. Reduce the heat and simmer for 20 minutes, until the lentils are soft and the dahl has a smooth consistency. Add the cabbage and cook for a further 5 minutes, stirring from time to time.

makes	suitable for	storage	preparation	nutritional value
3 child-sized servings	vegetarians; those intolerant to gluten, milk and lactose	24 hours in the refrigerator; 1 week in the freezer	10 minutes + 25 minutes cooking time	Good source of ★ iron ★ protein

To adapt either of these recipes for adults, add crushed garlic and chopped fresh green chilli to taste.

Corn Chowder

1 tsp good-quality vegetable oil or butter

5cm (2in) piece leek, well washed and sliced

¼ red pepper, finely chopped

300ml (½ pint) milk

125g (4oz) fresh, frozen or tinned sweetcorn (unsalted, unsweetened)

1 potato, chopped

1 bay leaf

60ml (2fl oz) single cream

Heat the oil or butter in a pan over medium heat. Gently fry the leek and red pepper until soft, about 5 minutes. Add the milk, sweetcorn, potato and bay leaf and bring to the boil.

Reduce the heat and simmer for 10 minutes or until the potato is tender. Add the cream, remove the bay leaf and blend briefly in a food processor or liquidizer.

A **CHOWDER** is a **THICK**, potato-based soup from America. This one contains **SWEETCORN** and **LEEK** and **CREAM** for added richness. Serve this with crusty bread or fingers of cheese on toast.

makes
6 child-sized servings

suitable for
vegetarians; those intolerant to gluten

storage
24 hours in the refrigerator; 1 week in the freezer

preparation
15 minutes

nutritional value
Good source of
★ complex carbohydrates
★ vitamin C

Burgers are one area where **VEGETARIAN** children often feel deprived. These bean burgers can be served with jacket potatoes and peas – or even covered with **TOMATO SAUCE** and served in a bun.

Spicy Bean Burgers

2 tbsp olive oil

1 onion, finely chopped

1 carrot, finely grated

1 green pepper, chopped

1 garlic clove, crushed

½ tsp ground coriander

½ tsp cumin seeds

2 x 400g (13oz) tin beans such as haricot, flageolet, kidney or chickpeas, rinsed and drained

1 tbsp tomato purée

1 egg, beaten

60g (2oz) dried breadcrumbs

60g (2oz) mature cheddar cheese, grated

salt and freshly ground black pepper

Preheat the oven to 200°C, 400°F, Gas 6.

Heat the oil in a frying pan over medium heat. Add the onion and fry gently until soft, about 5 minutes. Add the carrot, green pepper, garlic and spices and cook for a further 5 minutes. Remove from the heat.

In a large bowl, mash the beans and tomato purée together with a fork. Mix in the onion mixture, egg, breadcrumbs, cheese and seasoning. Divide the mixture into golf ball-sized portions and shape into burgers with your hands.

Place the burgers on an oiled baking sheet and bake in the oven until crisp, about 25 minutes. Turn the burgers half-way through cooking to crisp both sides.

makes	suitable for	storage	preparation	nutritional value
8 burgers	vegetarians	24 hours in the refrigerator; 1 week in the freezer	15 minutes + 25 minutes cooking time	Good source of ★ iron

The beans and egg in these burgers are a good source of iron in the vegetarian diet.

Mild Vegetable Korma with Couscous

1 tsp olive oil

1 small leek, well washed and sliced

½ tsp each ground cumin, garam masala and turmeric

1 carrot, diced

⅓ aubergine, chopped

1 small green pepper, diced

60g (2oz) small broccoli or cauliflower florets

60g (2oz) sliced mushrooms

60g (2oz) fresh or frozen baby broad beans

200ml (7fl oz) water or stock

2 tbsp tomato purée

60g (2oz) creamed coconut

125g (4oz) couscous or basmati rice

The **COCONUT** in this recipe mellows its **SPICINESS** and brings a delicious **CREAMINESS** to it; this is an ideal way to introduce your child to **NEW FLAVOURS**.

Heat the oil in a pan and fry the leek, cumin, garam masala and turmeric for 2 minutes. Add all the other ingredients, except the creamed coconut and couscous or rice and stir to mix.

Cover, bring to the boil, then reduce the heat and simmer, stirring occasionally, until the vegetables are tender, about 20 minutes.

Cook the couscous or rice according to the directions on the packet.

Stir the creamed coconut into the korma and heat for a further 2 minutes.

Arrange the couscous or rice into a ring shape, then spoon the korma into the middle of it to serve.

makes	suitable for	storage	preparation	nutritional value
4 child-sized servings	vegetarians; those intolerant to gluten, milk and lactose	24 hours in the refrigerator; 1 month in the freezer	10 minutes + 25 minutes cooking time	Good source of ★ iron ★ vitamin C

This is delicious served with naan or pitta bread and natural yoghurt mixed with cucumber pieces and chopped fresh mint.

Meat Burgers

500g (1lb) minced beef, lamb
or pork

1 small onion, finely chopped

½ tsp chopped fresh sage or
¼ tsp dried sage

60g (2oz) dried breadcrumbs

2 tsp good-quality vegetable oil,
if frying the burgers

These burgers can be fried or oven-cooked. If oven-cooking, preheat
the oven to 200°C, 400°F, Gas 6.

Mix the meat, onion, sage and breadcrumbs together in a bowl with
your hands.

Shape the mixture into satsuma-sized balls, then flatten into burgers.

If oven-cooking, place the burgers on a baking sheet and cook in
the oven for about 10–15 minutes, turning them half-way through
cooking. Test by inserting a skewer into the middle of a burger – there
should be no trace of pink in the meat and the juices should run clear.

If frying the burgers, heat the oil in a non-stick frying pan and fry over
medium heat until lightly browned, about 4 minutes on each side.
Again, when a skewer is inserted into the middle of a burger, there
should be no trace of pink in the meat and the juices should run clear.

Although fast food burgers are usually **TASTY**, you can't always be sure where the **INGREDIENTS** have come from. **HOME-MADE** burgers are a **TREAT** for children and are very **EASY** to prepare. Serve in a crusty or seeded bun with rings of tomato and onion and plenty of salad.

makes	suitable for	storage	preparation	nutritional value
4 large quarter-pounder or 8 standard-size burgers	those intolerant to milk and lactose	24 hours in the refrigerator	20 minutes + 10 minutes cooking time	Good source of ★ iron ★ zinc

Enlist the help of older children when preparing these burgers – they will have lots of fun and enjoy their meal even more.

Chicken Dippers and Dipping Sauces

Provided they are not the only food your child eats, these **CHICKEN** dippers can be a **FUN** and nutritious addition to your repertoire. Serve them with potatoes and baked beans or **RICE** with stir-fried vegetables.

FOR TOMATO DIPPING SAUCE:

250g (8oz) fresh tomatoes, chopped, or tinned tomatoes

½ small onion, finely chopped

1 garlic clove, crushed

2 tsp honey

1 tsp cornflour mixed with 2 tbsp water

FOR BARBECUE DIPPING SAUCE:

Follow the recipe above, but substitute unsweetened pineapple or other tropical fruit juice for the water.

FOR CHICKEN DIPPERS:

250g (8oz) skinless, boneless chicken breast, cut into thin strips

1 tbsp cornflour

60g (2oz) wholemeal breadcrumbs

freshly ground black pepper

½ tsp paprika

1 small egg, beaten

a little good-quality vegetable oil, for frying

Put all the ingredients for your chosen sauce in a pan. Stir well to mix, then cover and bring to the boil. Reduce the heat and simmer, covered, for 10 minutes, stirring occasionally.

Uncover and simmer for a further 15 minutes, stirring occasionally, until thickened. Liquidize and sieve the sauce, then set aside.

Make the chicken dippers: dip the chicken strips in the cornflour, covering them completely, and shake to remove any excess flour. Mix the breadcrumbs, pepper and paprika together. Dip the chicken strips in the egg, then roll in the breadcrumb mixture until entirely coated.

Heat the oil in a non-stick frying pan and fry the chicken strips over a medium heat for 10–15 minutes, turning them at least once, until golden on both sides.

makes	suitable for	storage	preparation	nutritional value
10 dippers	those intolerant to milk and lactose	sauce keeps for 3 days in the refrigerator; dippers should be eaten immediately	10 minutes + 15 minutes cooking time	Good source of ★ iron

To make home-made fish fingers, substitute 5cm (2in) chunks of a firm fish such as cod, haddock or salmon for the chicken.

This is a delicious way of serving **FRUIT** – hot and soft, it has **CRISPY BITS** but no added sugar. Serve this with **NATURAL YOGHURT** and a sprinkling of **NUTS**.

Summer Baked Fruit

1 eating apple, cored and roughly chopped

1 pear, cored and roughly chopped

segments from 1 small orange, halved

1 nectarine or peach, stoned and roughly chopped

1 banana, sliced

2 tbsp unsweetened orange or grapefruit juice

½ tsp cinnamon

Preheat the oven to 180°C, 350°F, Gas 4.

Place all the fruit in a shallow ovenproof dish. Add the orange or grapefruit juice and toss to coat the fruit. Sprinkle the cinnamon over the top.

Cover the dish with foil and bake in the oven, stirring occasionally, until the fruit is soft, about 20 minutes.

Remove the foil and crisp the surface of the fruit by baking for a further 15 minutes.

makes	suitable for	storage	preparation	nutritional value
3 child-sized servings	vegetarians; those intolerant to gluten, milk and lactose	24 hours in the refrigerator	10 minutes + 35 minutes cooking time	Good source of ★ vitamin C

This makes a light, delicate summer pudding, but would also make a wonderful breakfast treat served cold.

Wholemeal Pancakes

900ml (1½ pints) milk or buttermilk

3 eggs, beaten

60g (2oz) good-quality vegetable oil or melted butter

175g (6oz) plain white flour

175g (6oz) plain wholemeal flour

1 tsp cinnamon

125g (4oz) sultanas, raisins, dried cranberries or sour cherries

a little good-quality vegetable oil, for frying

Beat together the milk or buttermilk, eggs and oil or butter. Add the flour and cinnamon and beat until the batter is smooth, then leave to stand for 30 minutes. Stir in the dried fruit.

Heat a lightly oiled non-stick frying pan and pour in a small ladleful, about 3 tablespoons, of batter. Cook over medium heat until lightly browned, about 2–3 minutes on each side.

Children love these nutritious pancakes **ROLLED** up, **FOLDED** or eaten **FLAT**. They are great served with bananas, kiwis or peaches and cream cheese, or **HONEY** and **YOGHURT**.

makes	**suitable for**	**storage**	**preparation**	**nutritional value**
15–20 pancakes	vegetarians	best eaten immediately	45 minutes + 20 minutes cooking time	Good source of ★ calcium ★ iron

Try making

something different

for a weekend

BREAKFAST or a

TEA-TIME TREAT.

These **MOIST**

muffins have a

DISTINCTIVE TASTE

and **SMELL** that

many children love.

Raisin Bran Muffins

300g (10oz) unsweetened organic bran cereal

300g (10oz) wholemeal flour

2 tsp baking powder

2 large eggs, beaten

125ml (4fl oz) good-quality vegetable oil

125ml (4fl oz) molasses or black treacle, or 60ml (2fl oz) honey and 60ml (2fl oz) molasses or black treacle

300ml (½ pint) milk

125g (4oz) raisins or sultanas

Preheat the oven to 180°C, 350°F, Gas 4.

Combine the cereal, flour and baking powder in a large bowl.

In a separate bowl, blend the eggs, oil and molasses, treacle or honey milk and raisins or sultanas.

Mix all the ingredients together, stirring just until mixed.

Spoon the mixture into greased muffin tins, making sure not to fill them more than two-thirds full. Bake until golden and starting to come away from the sides of the tin, about 25–30 minutes.

makes	suitable for	storage	preparation	nutritional value
12 muffins	vegetarians	4 days in an airtight container	10 minutes + 25–30 minutes cooking time	Good source of ★ calcium ★ magnesium ★ potassium

Muffin tins are usually available from cook shops; if you can't find them, use paper cupcake cases and bake for just 15 minutes.

The idea is **SIMPLE** – take the most **DELICIOUS FRUITS** you can find, just **RIPE** and ready to eat, and blend them with **CRUSHED ICE** for **SMOOTHIES** or **MILK** for **MILKSHAKES**.

Fresh and Fruity Shakes

300ml (½ pint) milk*, or freshly squeezed juice of 2 oranges

½ glass crushed ice (ice cubes crushed with a rolling pin)

FOR BANANA SHAKE:
add 1 sliced banana

FOR PEAR SHAKE:
add 1 cored and chopped pear

FOR BERRY SHAKE:
add 1 handful strawberries, raspberries, blackberries or blueberries, or a combination

FOR PEACH SHAKE:
add 1 stoned and chopped ripe peach or nectarine

*rice, soy and follow-on milks may be substituted

Put the milk or orange juice and crushed ice in a blender. Add the fruit of your choice.

Blend the mixture at high speed until smooth, thick and bubbly.

Pour into glasses and serve immediately.

makes	suitable for	storage	preparation	nutritional value
1 serving	vegetarians; those intolerant to gluten	best drunk immediately	5 minutes	Good source of ★ vitamin C

These healthy shakes are full of nutrients and are an ideal way to encourage your child to enjoy fresh fruit.

Meal planners
4–7 months

When to wean is an important decision. Please see page 29 for important advice. Start with single flavour purées, then try him with the more varied recipes suggested for this age group. Once your baby can take food from a spoon, offer second and third meals at two-weekly intervals.

	BREAKFAST	MID A.M.	LUNCH	MID P.M.	SUPPER	BEDTIME
from weaning	Breast milk or formula milk	Breast milk or formula milk	Breast milk or formula milk	Breast milk or formula milk	3 tsp baby rice mixed with breast or formula milk	Breast milk or formula milk
after 2 weeks	3 tsp baby rice mixed with breast or formula milk	Breast milk or formula milk	Breast milk or formula milk	Breast milk or formula milk	2 tbsp puréed eating apple	Breast milk or formula milk
after 4 weeks menu 1	2 tbsp baby rice mixed with breast or formula milk	Breast milk or formula milk	Baby's First Vegetables*	Breast milk or formula milk	Fruit Compote*	Breast milk or formula milk
menu 2	Apple and Apricot Purée*	Breast milk or formula milk	Potato, carrot and broccoli purée	Breast milk or formula milk	Banana and Berries*	Breast milk or formula milk

*recipe included in book, see Index

7–10 months

During this stage your baby will be enjoying three meals a day and will have tried a range of foods. Now offer breast or formula milk after food, rather than before it, especially at breakfast time – milk will take the edge off your baby's appetite if given before solid food. You should now introduce iron-rich foods such as meat, fish, pulses and leafy green vegetables. These foods provide your baby with iron and protein as well as a range of minerals and vitamins needed to aid growth.

	BREAKFAST	MID A.M.	LUNCH	MID P.M.	SUPPER	BEDTIME
menu 1	Prune and Apple Porridge*	Breast milk or formula milk	Tomato and Cheese Sauce with Pasta*	Breast milk or formula milk	Fruity Rice with Chicken and Apricot* *or* Baby's First Vegetables*	Breast milk or formula milk
menu 2	Apple and Banana Breakfast*	Breast milk or formula milk	Sweetcorn and Potato*	Breast milk or formula milk	Tomato and Chicken Casserole* *or* Potato and Cheese Dinner*	Breast milk or formula milk
menu 3	Banana and Fig Porridge*	Breast milk or formula milk	Vegetable and Coconut Korma*	Breast milk or formula milk	Bolognese Sauce with Pasta* *or* Broccoli gratin	Breast milk or formula milk
menu 4	Banana and Mango Coulis*	Breast milk or formula milk	Mediterranean Vegetables and Chicken*	Breast milk or formula milk	Tomato and Basil Sauce with Pasta	Breast milk or formula milk
menu 5	Apricot Porridge*	Breast milk or formula milk	Poached fish and potato and broccoli purée	Breast milk or formula milk	Cauliflower cheese	Breast milk or formula milk

*recipe included in book, see Index

10–15months

Your baby will now have a well-established mealtime pattern. Babies are happiest when secure in a routine. This is the age to eat food with the family – your baby may well enjoy sharing your meal with you, and much of the food he eats will be suitable for the whole family. He will need about a pint of milk by now, including milk used in cooking and in milk products such as cheese and yoghurt.

	BREAKFAST	LUNCH	SUPPER
menu 1	Breakfast Surprise*	Creamy Mushroom Sauce with Pasta*	Mini Meatballs in Herby Tomato Sauce* *or* Sweetcorn and Potato* Baked Bananas*
menu 2	Mixed Fruit Compote*	Pumpkin Stew-in-a-Pot* *or* Tomato and Basil Sauce with Pasta*	Jacket Potato with Avocado Dip* Rice Pudding with Apricots*
menu 3	Apricot Porridge*	Fishy Rissoles* *or* Vegetable and Coconut Korma*	Tomato and Chicken Casserole* *or* Sweetcorn and Potato* Banana and Mango Coulis*
menu 4	Scrambled Egg with Wholemeal Toast	Beef Casserole* *or* Days Out Cakes* with mashed boiled egg	Jacket Potato with Dahl* Berries and Cherries*
menu 5	Apple and Banana Breakfast*	Dahl with rice*	Fishy Rissoles* *or* Tomato and Cheese Sauce with Pasta* Fresh fruit

*recipe included in book, see Index

Toddler

Toddlers like to graze and snack, and they need the frequent bursts of energy provided by snacks to fuel their growth and development. A slice of organic bread is more nutritious than a sweet biscuit, and a banana is a more suitable energy-rich food than a packet of crisps. Water is the best drink, but for variety, you could try fresh organic fruit juice diluted with water (one part juice to two parts water).

	BREAKFAST	LUNCH	SUPPER
menu 1	Apple and Orange Breakfast*	Roasted Butter Bean Gratin*	Mediterranean Lamb* *or* Fishy Rissoles* Mixed Fruit Compote*
menu 2	Baked beans and mushrooms on wholemeal toast	Jacket Potato with chicken, red and green peppers and butter* *or* with Hummus*	Sausages with Mash and Gravy* *or* Tomato and Basil Sauce with Pasta* Italian Bread and Butter Pudding*
menu 3	Banana and grapefruit segments Toast with butter	Pumpkin Stew-in-a-Pot* *or* Creamy Mushroom Sauce with Pasta*	Beef Casserole* *or* Vegetable and Coconut Korma* Fruit Bread Fingers,* yoghurt and chopped strawberries
menu 4	Boiled egg with rye bread toast	Avocado Dip* with pitta bread and Energy! Energy!* or other salad	Fruity Rice with Chicken and Apricot* (not puréed) with Barbecue Corn on the Cob* Berries and Cherries*
menu 5	Porridge with chopped fruit	Jacket Potato with brussels sprouts, tuna fish and a little olive oil*	Dahl with pitta bread* Fresh fruit salad

*recipe included in book, see Index

Preschool

This is the age of conformity. Children want to be like their peers, but also want to be part of the family. It is good to share one meal a day, even if it is simply an after-school snack (see opposite).

You can continue to influence your child's eating habits by keeping nutritious healthy food in the cupboard and fridge and making meals a time of relaxation and pleasure.

	BREAKFAST	LUNCH	SUPPER
menu 1	Grilled bacon with tomato and mushrooms and wholemeal toast	Little Gourmet Macaroni Cheese* with Energy! Energy!* or other salad	Sausages with Mash and Gravy* or Jacket Potato with Dahl* Summer Baked Fruit*
menu 2	Apple and Orange Breakfast* Toast	Corn Chowder* with Cheese on toast	Chicken Dippers and Dipping Sauces* or Fishy Rissoles* with mixed salad Wholemeal Pancakes*
menu 3	Wholemeal cereal and plain live yoghurt with banana and satsuma	Meat Burgers* or Spicy Bean Burgers* with home-made coleslaw	Mild Vegetable Korma with Couscous* Rice Pudding with Apricots*
menu 4	Boiled egg with wholemeal toast	Baked sweet potato with onion, mushroom, courgette and goat's cheese*	Mini Meatballs in Herby Tomato Sauce* or Creamy Mushroom Sauce with Pasta* Mixed Fruit Compote*
menu 5	Wholemeal Pancakes*	Fishy Rissoles* or Dahl with rice*	Tomato and Basil Sauce with Pasta* Raisin Bran Muffin*

*recipe included in book, see Index

Food for all occasions

quick fixes

Asterisked recipes take 15 minutes or less, others take 20 minutes or less.

It takes no time at all to prepare healthy and delicious food that your child will enjoy. The secret is a well stocked storecupboard.

4–7 months:
- Apple and Apricot Purée
- Fruit Compote
- Banana and Berries*
- Fruity Porridges* (Banana Porridge, Prune and Apple Porridge or Apricot Porridge)

7–10 months:
- Apple and Banana breakfast
- Banana and Fig Porridge*
- Rice Pudding with Apricots*

10–15 months:
- Mixed Fruit Compote*
- Creamy Mushroom Sauce with Pasta*
- Avocado Dip*
- Scrambled or boiled eggs with toast*
- Beans on wholemeal toast*

Toddler:
- Apple and Orange Breakfast*
- Sausages with Mash and Gravy*
- Hummus*
- Energy! Energy!*

Preschool:
- Corn Chowder*
- Fresh and Fruity Shakes*

snacks

Avoid highly processed snack foods which are high in sugar, fat and salt. There are plenty of tasty and nutritious alternatives.

- Fresh fruit such as apples, banana, grapes, kiwi fruit, mangoes, nectarines, peaches, pears, berries and satsumas cut into manageable pieces or chopped and served with yoghurt
- Dried fruit
- Juices
- Rice crackers (unsalted varieties)
- Wholemeal toast with butter or cheese
- Sprouting alfalfa, chickpeas, lentils, mung beans etc.
- Mini rice cakes, pitta breads and breadsticks
- Cherry tomatoes and vegetable sticks such as carrots, celery and cucumber served with dips such as hummus, avocado dip or yoghurt with chopped cucumber and mint

family meals

Remember to remove your child's portion before adding salt or hot spices. Be aware of the need for different textures at different ages.

- Mediterranean Vegetables and Chicken
- Tomato and Basil Sauce with Pasta
- Bolognese Sauce with Pasta
- Tomato and Cheese Sauce with Pasta
- Vegetable and Coconut Korma
- Fruity Rice with Chicken and Apricot
- Rice Pudding with Apricots
- Fishy Rissoles
- Beef Casserole
- Mini Meatballs in Herby Tomato Sauce
- Pumpkin Stew-in-a-Pot
- Baked Bananas
- Roasted Butter Bean Gratin
- Sausages with Mash and Gravy
- Mediterranean Lamb
- Barbecue Corn on the Cob
- Italian Bread and Butter Pudding
- Little Gourmet Macaroni Cheese
- Dahl
- Spicy Bean Burgers
- Mild Vegetable Korma with Couscous
- Meat Burgers
- Summer Baked Fruit

party food

This is food that children can have fun with. Your child might like to help you decorate cakes or muffins with fresh fruit.

- Days Out Cakes
- Fruit Bread Fingers
- Spicy Cheese and Potato Sticks
- Raisin Bran Muffins
- Fresh and Fruity Shakes
- Fruity Birthday Cakelets

HEALTH
ISSUES
and NUTRITION

During pregnancy or while breast-feeding

it is particularly important to eat a healthy,

balanced diet as the nutrients that you eat

are passed on to your baby. Raising your

child on a vegetarian or vegan diet requires

careful planning, and you may also need to

adapt your child's diet to cope with digestive

or allergic problems.

Pregnancy *and* breast-feeding

A diet for optimum health

In the 1950s and 1960s, Dr Ancel Keys and colleagues studied the effects of diet on the health of over 12,000 men from around the world, including Greece, Italy, Croatia, Serbia, Japan, Finland, the Netherlands and the US. The results showed that there was less heart disease in Mediterranean countries, and this is thought to be linked to their healthier diet. For instance, Mediterranean men eat less animal fat and far more complex carbohydrates such as pasta, bread and beans, than do men in northern Europe. The oil they eat is derived from olive oil or oily fish, and they eat large quantities of fresh fruit and vegetables, especially tomatoes.

As the same quality and variety of foods are readily available in Britain, anyone can adopt a similar pattern of eating, and this will meet all nutritional needs during pregnancy and while breast-feeding.

Why organic is important to the foetus

During pregnancy, good nutrition is doubly important because two people are reliant on one person's diet. Babies need to absorb not only all the nutrients they need from their mother's bloodstream, via the placenta, but also antibodies, which protect them from disease.

There is evidence that harmful substances can cross the placental barrier and affect the foetus. Even cigarette manufacturers now acknowledge the damage that tobacco can cause, and prospective parents are advised to stop smoking and to avoid smoky atmospheres. Alcohol can also be harmful in high doses. It can cause foetal alcohol syndrome, which produces abnormal physical and mental development.

DIET ESSENTIALS DURING PREGNANCY

Your baby eats what you eat. Consider the following guidelines for a healthy, balanced diet:

• Make fresh organic bread, pasta, pulses, potatoes and rice the foundation foods; they provide lots of energy as well as protein, vitamins and minerals

• Eat at least five servings of fresh fruit and vegetables a day

• Eat 60g (2oz) – 100g (3½oz) of protein a day; meat, fish, cheese, eggs and pulses are good sources

• Monitor fat intake: fat should constitute about 35% of your diet, with no more than 10% coming from animal sources; use olive oil for cooking and in dressings; eat oily fish twice a week to provide the Omega 3 oil important for building your baby's brain, eyes and nerves

• Include good sources of iron in your diet such as meat, fish, pulses, leafy green vegetables and wholegrains; half of your iron is absorbed by your baby.

It is reasonable to assume that the undesirable elements in conventional foods will be passed on to the growing embryo. As babies are at greater risk from pesticide residues, additives and toxins than are adults, it makes sense to avoid pesticides while you are pregnant.

The early weeks of pregnancy are a critical time as the baby's vital organs and limbs are forming. You can give your child the best possible start by eating plenty of wholesome, organic food.

Nutritional advice for expectant mothers

Because a pregnant woman's body ensures that her baby gets the nutrients it needs first, it is important to eat good, organic wholefoods that maintain your own health and vitality. Make sure that your diet is rich in minerals such as iron and calcium to prevent conditions such as anaemia and pregnancy-related osteoporosis. Calcium is best absorbed from natural sources (green vegetables, wholemeal bread, beans and lentils, for example) rather than supplements because excesses cannot be stored in the body. Vitamin D is essential as it helps the body to absorb calcium.

Folic acid deficiency needs to be avoided as this has been linked to spina bifida in babies. Supplements are recommended three months prior to conception and in the first three months of pregnancy, but you can also obtain folic acid from your diet. Many foods rich in folic acid are also rich in other essential nutrients. They include brussels sprouts, spinach, cauliflower, broccoli, cabbage, lettuce, green beans, peas, carrots, tomatoes, oranges, grapefruits, brown rice, potatoes and meat products. Be wary of breakfast cereals that are fortified with folic acid – they may be highly processed and high in sugar.

It is best to avoid raw eggs because of the risk of being infected with salmonella, and also pâté and soft cheese because of the risk of listeria. Try to eat a healthier diet and cut down on processed foods, as they are usually rich in cheap ingredients that are high in additives, sugar, fats and salt. Finally, reduce your caffeine intake and avoid artificial sweeteners – try to change your long-term diet to improve your own health as well as that of your baby.

A HEALTHY DIET DURING BREAST-FEEDING

What you eat can be passed on to your baby through your milk. If your diet lacks nutrients such as essential fats and zinc, your milk may lack these nutrients too. Follow these guidelines:

• Try to eat a good, balanced wholefood diet that includes plenty of fresh fruit, vegetables and fibre-rich foods

• Avoid stimulants such as alcohol and caffeine

• Avoid hot, spicy foods

• Drink at least 2 litres (3.5 pints) of fluids a day to replace the breast milk lost

• Tell your pharmacist or doctor that you are breast-feeding before they suggest any medicines for you.

The key to successful breast-feeding is plenty of rest and a varied diet of small, frequent meals.

the Vegetarian baby and child

PROTEINS FOR VEGANS AND VEGETARIANS

Proteins are made from amino acids and are important body builders, necessary for maintaining tissue and sustaining growth. The body manufactures much of the protein we need itself, the rest we get from food. Plant sources of protein can meet the body's needs just as well as animal sources. While vegetarians get protein from dairy products and eggs, vegans can derive it from the following sources:

• Nuts such as peanuts, almonds, brazil nuts and hazelnuts (see Essential Nutrients, opposite)

• Seeds such as pumpkin, sunflower and sesame

• Pulses and beans such as soya, lentils, chickpeas and kidney beans

• Wholegrains found in foods such as wholemeal bread and pasta, oats and wholegrain rice.

Ensuring a nutritionally balanced diet

It is estimated that three per cent of children in the UK follow a vegetarian or vegan diet. There are three types of vegetarian: those who simply exclude meat, poultry and fish from their diet; others who also exclude eggs; and vegans, who additionally exclude dairy products.

All of these choices mean that you must take more responsibility for ensuring that the diet is nutritionally balanced. Eating enough of the right nutrients in a meat-based diet is a relatively easy thing to do in most cultures because there is a wide choice of foods. But when you exclude foods from your diet, you need to know what impact this can have on your long-term health. Nowhere is this more important than in planning your child's diet – childhood is such a critical period of body building that it has an impact on your child's health for the rest of his life. Vegetarianism does not need to be associated with a reduction in choice – it often means a healthier and more varied diet. But it does need more care in its construction to ensure that it is life-enhancing.

Veganism

Of particular concern is veganism, because without careful planning it can be difficult to provide the nutrients essential for a growing child. You should breast-feed for at least the first year of your baby's life and take vitamin supplements, especially vitamin B12, which can be deficient in the vegan diet. If you choose to give your baby formula milk, there are soya-based varieties available, and you should feed your baby this for two years. Because soya formula milk is high in sugars, cup-feeding from six months is recommended to protect children's teeth, and you should aim to have your baby drinking from a cup by the age of one. By this age, offer milk at mealtimes only, and never before going to bed. Seek advice from a health professional before feeding soya-based baby formula to your baby.

Why organic food is so important

Vegans and vegetarians will especially benefit from organic fruits and vegetables because produce reaches the customer more quickly after harvesting, and therefore the nutrient content is likely to be higher than in non-organic produce. This is particularly the case with the less stable, water-soluble vitamins such as vitamin C. Research is beginning to demonstrate that because organic produce grows in accordance with its natural growth cycle, nourished by rich topsoil and not forced with artificial fertilizers and growth regulators, the mature fruit or vegetable is likely to have more solid matter rich in nutrients. Additionally, organic fruit and vegetables are not waxed to prolong their shelf-life, which means that there is less time for their nutrients to deteriorate.

Essential nutrients

Where possible, use whole versions of foods, for example wholegrain rice, as the nutrient content of these foods is likely to be higher than their refined counterparts. Vegetarian and vegan storecupboards can contain true convenience foods such as beans, legumes and whole grains. Cheese, dairy products and eggs are great energy foods for vegetarian babies. Vegans need to replace the nutrient-dense energy foods such as meat and eggs with a range of nuts and seeds and their oils and butters. Almond butter and tahini (sesame spread) are popular choices. However, some of these foods are known allergens (see pages 136–37) and there is controversy as to when they should be given to children. If there is a history of allergies in the family, whether it is asthma, eczema or a food allergy, discuss the weaning needs of your vegetarian or vegan baby with a health professional before you begin.

NUTRIENT DEFICIENCY RISKS

Bear the following nutrient deficiency risks in mind when planning meals for your vegetarian or vegan child:

• Iron and zinc: good sources are wholemeal bread, rice, oats, nuts, pulses, tofu, soya protein, miso, parsley and bean sprouts

• Vitamin B12: yeast extract, margarines and breakfast cereals are good sources

• Vitamin D: the best source is dairy products or the action of sunlight on the skin; vegans may need to take supplements

• Vitamin B2: mushrooms, fortified breakfast cereals and yeast extract are good sources

• Vitamin A: carrots, spinach, pumpkins, tomatoes, dark green vegetables and vegan margarine are good sources.

Parents can now choose from a range of 100% organic babyfoods, many of which are vegetarian or vegan.

Special diets *for* your child

HYPERACTIVITY

Children who are hyperactive have unusually short attention spans and are often excitable and impetuous. Hyperactivity may be the result of:

• Disruption of the brain chemistry

• Eating too many foods processed with refined carbohydrates and loaded with additives.

If you suspect that your child's hyperactivity may be related to diet, seek advice from a health professional who may advise taking the following steps:

• Replace any suspect foods with organic wholefood alternatives

• Keep a record of your child's diet and behaviour.

If this does not solve the problem, talk to your health professional again. He or she is trained to help with your child's behaviour and can refer you to experts who can provide you with support.

Common food allergies

Much has been written about food allergies, some of it alarmist and much of it contradictory. Words such as food intolerance, adverse reaction and hypersensitivity add to the mystery. Put simply, an allergy is where the body reacts to a harmless substance, such as a food, as if it was harmful. This can be very serious.

The allergic reaction

A baby can develop a reaction to a food in the uterus, via breast milk, or when he first eats the food. In an allergy, his body produces antibodies called immunoglobulins on first contact with the allergen (the food). When the food and antibodies meet again this triggers the allergic reaction, which can take the form of asthma, eczema, mouth or tongue swelling, hayfever, rash, diarrhoea or abdominal pain.

Reducing the risk

If your baby experiences this type of reaction, the allergen must be identified and excluded, as further contact could produce more intense reactions. A family history of allergies may double your child's risk of allergy, so seek a paediatric dietician's advice if this is the case. Breast-feeding for at least four to six months will provide your baby with protective antibodies. Foods known to be allergens should not be given until after six months of age. Conventional processed foods, which contain a plethora of additives, as well as possible artificial chemical and antibiotic residues, place extra pressure on the immune systems of sensitive babies. This can be avoided by opting for organic alternatives.

Common allergens

Foods commonly associated with allergies are cow's milk, eggs, nuts, wheat, strawberries, citrus fruits, fish, shellfish and sesame seeds. However, it is important that your child eats a wide variety of wholesome foods. Do not exclude foods on suspicion of allergy without talking to your doctor, because a restrictive diet can result in malnutrition.

Peanuts, and ingredients derived from them, are widely used in food processing which may be why this allergy is appearing more often. The UK government has advised that children should avoid peanuts before five years of age. Always read the labels to check that foods are nut-free.

Digestive problems

Diarrhoea, constipation, colic and posseting are common digestive problems that can cause much anxiety.

Gastroenteritis, a bowel inflammation caused by infection, is the commonest cause of diarrhoea and can be very serious in infants. It is important to get medical help as infants dehydrate quickly and lose essential nutrients. Diarrhoea can be a side effect of drugs, especially antibiotics, or it may be diet-related and indicate a lactose or gluten intolerance or even too much fibre or fruit juice in the diet. In these cases changes to the diet, where advised, will be effective.

Constipation can be painful and distressing. In bottle-fed babies it may be a sign that the milk is too concentrated. When the problem occurs in children who eat mainly processed foods, it can be resolved by adding wholemeal bread, fruit and vegetables to the diet.

Babies with colic draw up their legs in pain after a feed and cry loudly, sometimes for hours. Gentle rocking movements, such as pushing your baby in a pram may help, and baby massage can be effective.

Most babies posset, or regurgitate, small amounts of food after meals. Holding your baby still in a upright position after feeding may help, so might taking your baby's weight on one hand while gently massaging his back as this allows food to settle.

WEIGHT PROBLEMS IN BABIES

By the end of their first year, most babies will have tripled their birth weight. The following weight problems are generally quite rare in babies:

• Obesity

In the past, plump babies developed into muscular toddlers as they became more active. Today increasing numbers become obese. They eat more sugary, processed foods than ever before and are also more sedentary, preferring to watch television rather than play outside.

• Underweight babies

Some babies do not grow at a steady pace. There are organizations that can advise on suitable foods and quantities for underweight babies (see pages 140–41), or your GP may refer you to a paediatrician.

Introduce your baby to new foods one at a time so that the cause of any allergic reaction will be more obvious.

Seasonal produce guide

Choosing to eat seasonally should mean that you eat the freshest fruit and vegetables available as well as supporting your local rural economy. This chart will give you an idea of the produce to expect from an organic box scheme.

Fruits

	SPRING			SUMMER			AUTUMN			WINTER		
	EARLY	MID	LATE	EARLY	MID	LATE	EARLY	MID	LATE	EARLY	MID	LATE
Apples: Bramley								●	●		●	●
Cox							●	●	●	●	●	●
Discovery						●	●	●	●	●	●	●
Gala							●	●	●	●	●	●
Blackberries					●	●	●					
Cherries				●	●							
Pears: Comice	●	●						●	●			
Conference	●							●	●	●		
Plums							●	●	●			
Raspberries				●	●	●	●					
Strawberries				●	●	●		●				

Herbs

	EARLY	MID	LATE	EARLY	MID	LATE	EARLY	MID	LATE	EARLY	MID	LATE
Basil		●	●	●	●	●	●	●	●			
Chives		●	●	●	●	●	●	●	●	●		
Mint		●	●	●	●	●	●	●	●			
Parsley		●	●	●	●	●	●	●	●			
Rosemary	●	●	●	●	●	●	●	●	●		●	●
Sage		●	●	●	●	●	●	●	●			

Vegetables

Vegetables	Spring			Summer			Autumn			Winter		
	Early	Mid	Late	Early	Mid	Late	Early	Mid	Late	Early	Mid	Late
Aubergine			•	•	•	•	•					
Beans: Broad				•	•							
Runner				•	•	•	•	•				
Brussels sprouts	•						•	•	•	•	•	•
Cabbage: Red	•	•	•	•	•	•	•	•	•	•	•	•
Spring greens	•	•	•	•					•	•	•	•
Savoy	•	•	•	•			•	•	•	•	•	•
White	•	•	•	•				•	•	•	•	•
Calabrese and broccoli			•	•	•	•	•	•	•			
Carrots				•	•	•	•	•	•	•		
Cauliflowers		•	•	•	•	•	•	•	•			
Celery			•			•	•	•				
Courgettes			•	•	•	•	•					
Cucumbers		•	•	•	•	•	•	•				
Leeks	•	•	•	•			•	•	•	•		•
Lettuce			•	•	•	•	•					
Mangetouts					•	•	•					
Marrows			•	•	•	•	•	•				
Parsnips	•						•	•	•	•	•	•
Peas			•	•	•	•	•	•	•			
Potatoes: Maincrop						•	•	•	•	•		
New			•	•								
Pumpkins						•	•	•	•	•	•	•
Purple sprouting broccoli		•	•									
Spinach				•	•	•	•	•				
Spring onions			•	•	•	•	•	•				
Swede							•	•	•	•	•	•
Sweet peppers				•	•	•	•	•				
Tomatoes			•	•	•	•						
Turnips							•	•	•	•	•	
Watercress	•	•	•	•	•	•	•	•	•			

Box schemes are a great way to learn about which fruit and vegetables are in season and when.

Useful addresses

environmental groups

FRIENDS OF THE EARTH
26–28 Underwood Street,
London N1 7JQ
0207 490 1555
www.foe.co.uk
The largest international network of environmental groups in the world.

GREENPEACE
Canonbury Villas,
London WC1N 3XX
0207 865 8100
www.greenpeace.org
Campaigns for a green and peaceful planet.

WOMEN'S ENVIRONMENTAL NETWORK
PO Box 30626,
London E1 1TZ
0207 481 9004
www.gn.apc.org/wen
Tackles environmental issues, especially those affecting women.

farm visits

FEDERATION OF CITY FARMS AND COMMUNITY GARDENS
The Greenhouse, Hereford Street,
Bedminster, Bristol BS3 4NA
0117 923 1800
www.farmgarden.org.uk
Information about city farms and community gardens in the UK.

HENRY DOUBLEDAY RESEARCH ASSOCIATION
Ryton Organic Gardens,
Coventry CV8 3LG
01203 303517
www.hdra.org.uk

ORGANIC FARM NETWORK
See Soil Association entry
for contact details
A nationwide project organized by the Soil Association that aims to show the public how organic farms work.

food safety

CONSUMERS' ASSOCIATION
2 Marylebone Road,
London NW1 4DF
0207 770 7000
www.which.net
Organization that protects the rights of the consumer.

FOOD COMMISSION
94 White Lion Street,
London N1 9PF
0207 837 2250
www.foodcomm.org.uk
The UK's leading independent watchdog on food issues.

MAFF HELPLINE
Ministry of Agriculture,
Fisheries and Foods
(MAFF),
3–8 Whitehall Place,
London SW1A 2HH
0645 335577
www.maff.gov.uk
Central contact point for government information on food issues.

PESTICIDE ACTION NETWORK UK
Eurolink Centre,
49 Effra Road,
London SW19 4EZ
0207 274 8895
www.pan-uk.org
An independent body working to eliminate the hazards of pesticides.

health matters

ANAPHYLAXIS CAMPAIGN
PO Box 149,
Fleet,
Hampshire GU13 9XU
01252 542029
www.anaphylaxis.org.uk

BRITISH ALLERGY FOUNDATION
Deepdene House,
30 Bellegrove Road,
Welling,
Kent GA16 3PY
0208 303 8583
www.allergyfoundation.com

BRITISH NUTRITION FOUNDATION

High Holborn House,
52–54 High Holborn,
London WC1V 6RQ
0207 404 6504
www.nutrition.org.uk

THE CHILDREN'S SOCIETY

Edward Rudolph House,
Margery Street,
London WC1X 0JL
0207 841 4400
Provides information about dealing with underweight babies.

COELIAC SOCIETY

PO Box 220, 1B Octagon Court,
High Wycombe,
Buckinghamshire HP11 2HY
01494 437278
www.coeliac.co.uk

FORESIGHT

28 The Paddocks,
Godalming,
Surrey GU7 1XD
01483 427839
www.surreyweb.org.uk./
foresight/home.html
Provides information on additives in food in relation to preconceptual care.

THE HYPERACTIVE CHILDREN'S SUPPORT GROUP

71 Whyke Lane,
Chichester,
West Sussex PO19 2LD
01903 725182

LA LECHE LEAGUE

LLL(GB),
PO Box 29, West Bridgford,
Nottingham NG2 7NP
0207 242 1278
www.stargate.co.uk
Provides breast-feeding support and information.

NATIONAL CHILDBIRTH TRUST

Alexandra House,
Oldham Terrace,
London W3 6NH
0207 992 8637
www.nat-online.org
Offers support in pregnancy, childbirth and early parenthood.

VEGAN SOCIETY

Donald Watson House,
7 Battle Road,
St Leonards on Sea,
East Sussex TN37 7AA
01424 427393
www.vegansociety.com

THE VEGETARIAN SOCIETY

Parkdale,
Dunham Road,
Altringham,
Cheshire WA14 4QG
0161 925 2000
www.vegsoc.org

organic food suppliers and box schemes

CLEARSPRING DIRECT

Acton Park Estate,
London W3 7QE
0208 749 1781
www.clearspring.co.uk
UK-wide home delivery of wide range of wholefoods.

EASTBROOK FARM ORGANIC MEATS

Bishopstone,
Swindon,
Wiltshire SN6 8PW
01793 790469
UK-wide home delivery of organic meat.

JEKKA'S HERB FARM

Rose Cottage,
Shellards Lane,
Alveston,
Bristol BS35 3SY
01454 418 878
www.jekkasherb.demon.co.uk
Provides mail-order herb seeds and plants to grow at home.

ORGANICS DIRECT

1/7 Willow Street,
London EC2A 4BH
0207 729 2828
www.organicsdirect.com
UK-wide home delivery of wide range of organic produce.

ORGANIX

Freepost BH1 336, Christchurch,
Dorset BH23 2ZZ
0800 393511
www.babyorganix.co.uk

PLANET ORGANIC

42 Westbourne Grove,
London W2 5SH
0207 727 2227
www.planetorganic.com
Natural food and organic supermarket with local delivery.

SOIL ASSOCIATION

Bristol House,
40–56 Victoria Street,
Bristol BS1 6BY
0117 9142400
www.soilassociation.org
The UK's leading campaigning and certification body for organic food and farming. Provides directory of organic food suppliers for a small fee.

SWADDLES GREEN ORGANIC FARM

Hare Lane, Buckland St Marys,
Chard, Somerset TA20 3JR
01460 234387
www.swaddles.co.uk
Organic meat by mail order.

Index

Figures in **bold** indicate recipes.

Acknowledgments

AUTHOR'S APPRECIATION

Many people have made this book possible: Mike Thrasher, Zoe Letts, Kim
Teal, Marie Van Hagen and especially Mary Daly and Jackie Gray at Organix
all contributed ideas, time and hard work to the researching and writing of it
– even over Christmas!
Professor John Wargo of the Department of Environmental Sciences
at Yale University; Dr Vyvyan Howard, Paediatric Toxicologist
at the University of Liverpool; Dr Michael Crawford at the
Institute of Brain Chemistry; Betsy Lydon at Mothers &
Others, New York; Patrick Holden, Policy Director at the
Soil Association; Tim Lobstein and Sue Dibb of the Food
Commission; Joanna Blythman; Suzannah Olivier; Michael
Van Straten and health visitors nationwide have all inspired
key sections of the book. The work they do on behalf of
children's health inspires and motivates all of us
at Organix every day.
Thanks to my mother and father, Richard and Betty Vann,
for sharing their determination to achieve goals and their
love of good food at an early age; Lynda Brown for her
good ideas and Derek Cooper and Nigel Slater for talking
and writing about good food in such a mouthwatering
way – an inspiration to us all!

And finally, thanks to everyone at Dorling Kindersley for making this book what
it is. Especially to Nasim Mawji, my editor, for her enormous patience and
persistence when nothing seemed to be happening and to Simon Brown
and the design team for making this book so attractive. And, of course, to
Rosemary Scuolar at PFD for making it happen!

Dorling Kindersley would like to thank the National Farmers'
Union for the Seasonal Produce Guide; Liz Bauwens for
styling; Angela Haldane for photographic assistance; Valerie
Lewis Chandler for the index. Thanks to the following for
kindly loaning equipment and props: Bombay Duck, London;
The Conran Shop, London; Eccentrics (mail order); Geoffrey
Drayton, London; Urchin (mail order). Thanks to our models:
Jamie Banghard, Joseph Belcher, Finn Brown, Georgina Caine,
Alex Calver, Amirah Chiori, Luisa Cross, Emily Davis, Ardan
Devine, Chen Dew, Myfanwy Dew, Christian El-Shamma, Star
Epiphany, Paschal Golding, Tariq Jogee, Robert King, Finlay
Mackenzie, Lily Marr-Johnson, Lily McCarthy, Jasper Morley,
Max Napier, Eloise Newton, Morgan Oxley-King, Max
Ridley, Ruby Ridley, Cheiko Sato, Natalie Shepherd, George
Stephenson, Tomos Vaughan-Streater, Jasper Watt, Kathryn
Watt and Kate Wilson.